When Food Is Your Best Friend

(AND WORST ENEMY)

When Food Is Your Best Friend

(AND WORST ENEMY)

Jan Johnson

HarperSanFrancisco
A Division of HarperCollins*Publishers*

Unless otherwise noted, all scripture quotations are from the Holy Bible, New International Version. Copyright © 1973, 1978, 1984 International Bible Society. Used by permission of Zondervan Bible Publishers.

Selected names and circumstances of anecdotes in this text have been changed to retain the anonymity of those who shared their lives with the author.

Permissions continued on page 246.

FIRST EDITION

Library of Congress Cataloging-in-Publication Data

Johnson, Jan.
When food is your best friend (and worst enemy) / Jan Johnson.—1st ed.
p. cm.
Includes bibliographical references.
ISBN 0–06–064252–1 (pbk.)
1. Compulsive eaters—Religious life. 2. Compulsive eating—Religious aspects—Christianity. 3. Johnson, Jan, 1952–. I. Title.
BV4596.C58J64 1993 92–54534
248.8'6—dc20 CIP

93 94 95 96 97 98 RRD(H) 10 9 8 7 6 5 4 3 2

This edition is printed on acid-free paper that meets the American National Standards Institute Z39.48 Standard.

To my lover, friend, and life partner, Greg,
who watched my struggle and chose to
believe in me.

Contents

Acknowledgments

I am grateful to my partners in this project:

those who provide such good examples to me in recovery: Jeff, Dan, Cheryl, and Dana;

those who reviewed the manuscript: therapist Charlene Underhill, writer Dana Mildebrath, and, as always, my husband, Greg Johnson;

my writer-editor friend Gloria Chisholm, who first saw this book within me and urged me to write it;

Lonnie Hull, then editor at Harper San Francisco, who, after I had backed off from this dream and buried it, not only resurrected the dream but also set forth a purpose and a tone for this book that I immediately recognized as God's will for me and could not let go of.

In keeping with its tradition of nonaffiliation, Overeaters Anonymous has not endorsed this or any other book.

INTRODUCTION

One Beggar Telling Another . . .

Have you ever wanted to take a long walk with a recovering compulsive eater and hear about the ups and downs of recovery? What made it work? you might ask the recovering person. What almost foiled it? Books that simulate that kind of walk instigated my recovery and prodded me to keep going. I've remembered the authors' stories, and I've imagined myself walking in their footsteps.

This book is an opportunity for you to take a walk with me to hear an insider's version of recovering from compulsive overeating. I'd like to show you some of the beautiful sights along the way, and I want to offer you some perspectives to remember when you fall. I want you to know that others have gone before you and have found a life that is full of serenity, purpose, and even fun.

My struggle includes many years of compulsive eating and several years of recovery. I've spent a lot of time in the rooms of Overeaters Anonymous and various church-related eating disorder support groups. As I've written magazine articles about recovery, I've interviewed many therapists and psychologists, and I've included their insights along the way.

This book does not address fitness and nutrition needs, and I encourage you to investigate those areas if you haven't done so. This book doesn't take the place of attending support groups or therapy or even treatment center experiences if those are needed. It provides a look at the inner journey of the compulsive eater working on recovery.

WHY WRITE FROM A FAITH PERSPECTIVE?

I could not write on this subject from any perspective other than a spiritual, specifically Christian, one because it seemed useless to me to write a book with information about "how to" but not about the "power to" overcome. My compulsive overeating has sabotaged my life-long struggle to know God, and recovery has helped me feel loved by God and become eager to follow him. I find my path similar to that of Thomas Kelly, one of the great devotional masters, who "knew that he was himself brought to his final level of hunger [for God] by his need to face a cleft in himself and by God flooding into him in a way that was both unpredictable and unpreparable."[1]

Although I loved God and was a leader in my church, I was also hooked on compulsive eating. As my despair with God grew and I felt weary of being a Christian, I faced that fractured cleft in myself (my compulsive overeating) and tumbled into recovery. Since then God has flooded into my life in unpredictable and unorthodox ways. I am finally more hungry for God than I have ever been.

Many of us who have followed the Twelve Steps have had this experience. We saw scriptural principles in them and followed them in that light. Our recovery released us to God in a new and different way—we finally turned ourselves over to him.

EVERY JOURNEY IS DIFFERENT

This is not a book of formulas, because formulas are controlling, not freeing. They convince us that we've found "the solution"! Then we try to use this solution, but it doesn't work because we're all different. The Twelve Steps aren't a formula but a general, loose path that we can follow according to our temperament and the way God chooses to deal with us. That's the key: surrendering ourselves to God, not to a formula.

Your walk of recovery will probably differ in many ways from mine because God interacts with us in custom-made ways. However, know that if you try to address your compulsive eating without the faith dimension, without self-examination, surrender, and rigorous honesty, you risk transferring your compulsive eating to some other, perhaps more subtle, compulsion.

One more clarification, please. My study of the Bible leads me to believe that since God's image is both male and female (Gen. 1:27), God's personhood encompasses both male and female. Even though I see God this way, I have followed the traditional path of referring to God with masculine pronouns. I trust that "he" understands this limited way of referring to "him," and I hope you do, too.

PART ONE

What Is My Problem?

ONE

Hungry for Something More

Some people do not understand what I mean when I say that food was my best friend, but perhaps you will. Meet Nancy, Kathy, and Brenda.[1] They understand.

NANCY, HUNGRY FOR COMFORT

It was prom night, and everything seemed magical for a few moments. My date was a nice boy who was also funny. We enjoyed each other at the dance, but on the way to an after-prom party, he pulled out a bottle of beer. When we parked at the house where the party was, he leaned over and began pulling at my dress. I screamed, and he yelled at me.

We hurried into the house, where I hid in the laundry room. I tried to think of whom I could call. Not my parents, that's for sure. I opened the door and wandered over to the snack table. I saw my date dancing very close with another girl, so I retreated to the laundry room, grabbing a bag of chips as I went. I remember smearing the salt and grease from my hands across my face and hoping my face would break out in pimples.

A little later, the mother of the girl who was having the party came into the laundry room and asked if I was OK. We talked for a few minutes, and she offered to take me home.

"Oh, no, you don't have to do that," I replied.

"I have to buy more soda anyway. I'll drop you off," she said, so I agreed.

The next morning my parents asked how it went, and I told them that everything was fine. My mother suggested that the boy might call again, but I assured her he wouldn't. She didn't ask why.

That wasn't the first time that I felt as if the word *victim* were written on my forehead and some sharp person read it. I could barely remember, of course, but it was there, standing between my parents and me. When I was about five, my father began visiting me in my bedroom at night and playing sexual games with me. I hated it, but I didn't know what to do. He told me not to tell my mother, but why didn't she hear? He would laugh and yell so loud!

When I was about nine or ten, he stopped. Then I became afraid he would start molesting my little sister. One time he looked as if he was coming after her, and I grabbed the biggest kitchen knife we had. I stood in the bedroom doorway and yelled at him. His eyes got big, and he left the room. He must have told my mother about the knife, because she came in and scolded me for having it. I looked at her with disgust and put the knife away. Later I took another one and kept it under my bed for years. I think my father knew that touching my sister would be the one thing that would make me not live up to the pet name my parents had given me, "Mouse."

At home, I spent most of my time zoned out in front of the television hugging a bag of cookies as if it were a teddy bear. I made friends at school, but I never felt close to anyone—or, rather, I never let them get close to me.

I ended up marrying Clint, a nice guy who didn't bother me much about anything. I knew he wanted me to enjoy sex, but how was that supposed to happen? I did enjoy the closeness, however, so I did my "sexual duty."

I liked my job. I supervised a busy office, and we used any excuse to have potluck lunches. I saw the weight coming on, but I wasn't too heavy, so I didn't worry. My problems began when a friend who attended support group meetings told me that she depended on food. Listening to her made me realize how much I loved food—my only friend and companion. I went to meetings with her, but when I would try to stop eating, I was filled with fear and anger. I became obsessed with what my father had done to me, so I wound up eating before and after every meeting.

I decided to go into therapy. This baffled Clint, but he came with me, and we talked about my anger toward my dad (and toward my mom, who I'm sure knew about the sexual abuse and refused to protect me). As I progressed, I went back to the compulsive overeating support group, and it wasn't so scary then.

Clint came with me to therapy the day I confronted my dad in an imaginary way. I shouted, "I am not a bad person, and I don't want to. . . . " Shortly after that, my parents came to visit. My dad criticized my new stylish shoes and suggested I throw them away.

I whirled around, and the same words came out: "I am not a bad person, and I don't want to . . . throw these shoes away."

My father flinched and looked offended. I could feel Clint standing behind me, as if he were going to catch me if I fainted. This gave me the courage to confront my father about the abuse. He stood there for a while and then said to my mom, "Shall we be going?"

My parents pretend that the talk never took place, but it made a big difference in me. I acknowledged the truth, and it's easier for me to see the truth in myself, too. I wrote a Twelve-Step inventory (a history of my compulsion and character defects) and realized that I've used the abuse as an excuse to feel sorry for myself all my life and that I've distanced myself from people.

I have confessed to my support group that I have been mad at God and everyone else for years and that I am finally willing to surrender my anger. I feel that I can finally trust people, and God, too. I'm trying to turn my need for food over to God and allow him to comfort me. Now no one holds power over me unless I give it to them, and I'm giving God more of that power every day.

KATHY, HUNGRY FOR CONTROL

I sat in the lobby watching the people walk into the auditorium for the therapists' convention. No one I knew had arrived, and since this was my first year to attend, I wanted to sit with someone who knew the ropes.

I looked at my watch: twenty-five minutes until the program began. I found the snack bar and ordered a large diet soda. Then, after checking to make sure none of my colleagues had popped in, I grabbed a candy bar. As the cashier rang up my purchases, I threw two more candy bars on the counter. I rushed into the women's bathroom, stood in a stall, and scarfed down two of the candy bars and gulped my diet soda. Then I came out, checked my face in the mirror for chocolate smudges, brushed off my suit, and stuck the other candy bar in my purse. *I may need this later,* I thought.

I strolled back to the auditorium, trying to appear relaxed as I sipped my diet soda. By the time I saw a colleague, I felt confident and ready to face the world.

That's how my life used to be—all the time. Food became my best friend when I was twelve. My overweight parents fought constantly. Sometimes I buried my head in my pillow and cried; other times I sat on the stairway and listened as if I were the scorekeeper at a ball game.

After my parents went to bed, I used to sneak downstairs and get a snack. I especially liked to make tunafish salad. (There was no junk food in our house, thanks to my mom, who dieted constantly.) Then I'd take my bowl of tunafish upstairs and eat it all. Soon I would be calm enough to go to sleep. In a month's time, candy wrappers, assorted plates, and several bowls of dried tunafish would collect under my bed.

I comfortably absorbed the extra calories until I was in college. Then I saw that I was gaining weight, so I went on my first diet. I counted calories and lost the weight. Control was no problem for me.

It wasn't as easy after I got married. Trying to get along with someone meant I had to keep my refrigerator stocked with things that pacified my bad moods. Every fall I gained fifteen or twenty pounds and dieted it away in the spring so I could look decent in a swimsuit. I joined health spas and diet clubs. Over the years I built up an entire library of diet books, and I could make any recipe using nonfat milk, low-calorie sweetener, or half as much oil.

It got more difficult to lose the weight each time, and I felt more grouchy, as if my life were in a holding pattern of emptiness until I finished the diet. I became moody and critical of my husband, and after several years he left me. I was working through that when I heard about a support group meeting for overeaters at a church near my office—but how could I, a therapist and a leader at my own church, join those people?

Still I kept dieting until, one time in a fit of anger, I yelled at a client. The client left and never came back. Then I realized that I picked on everyone I knew—friends, family, even the pastor. The worse I felt, the more I ate. I knew I was out of control.

After a few therapy sessions for myself, I decided to try the support group. On the way, I stopped for a hamburger and fries, and then I changed into some old sweat clothes. I put my hair in a ponytail and washed off my makeup. No one would ever recognize me! I even used my full first name, Kathleen.

I heard people talk at the meeting about their love affair with food, and I thought, *At last I'm home!* I tried what they called abstinence, but I binged every time I was upset or lonely.

I heard about "sponsors" and laughed at the thought. I was a therapist—how could I have a sponsor? Besides, no one seemed good enough.

Finally, I went out for coffee afterward with a crusty older woman named Margaret. I didn't like her that much, but she was tough and honest. As we talked, I felt as if she saw right through me, but she had a tender side, too. She talked about surrendering, and I found that hard.

"If I quit controlling my eating, I'll binge like crazy," I told her.

She laughed. "You've been controlling it, and you binge anyway."

Cheap shot, I thought.

After that I started devouring literature on compulsive eating, and it seemed like a strange approach: become empowered by letting go.

After that, I called Margaret whenever I was mad. We went round and round. "Who says you have to be so wonderful?" Margaret cornered me one time. So I spilled it: "Nothing ever satisfied my mother. I remember filling a bucket with weeds, like she said, and then she mashed them down and told me to pull more. She always made it clear that I wasn't good enough."

The next morning, I realized I'd made an error in my checkbook, and I flew into a rage at myself. I saw how I put myself down as much as or more than my mom ever had.

I finally wrote an inventory, which I read to Margaret. I couldn't look up as I read, but I could hear her crying.

"I've had all these feelings, and I've done the same things, Kathleen," Margaret said. "I'm glad you wrote about them."

The next day I called the client I had yelled at. I told him that I had been wrong to yell at him and that I was working some things out for myself. He seemed confused, thanked me, and hung up, but I felt much better.

The next time I tried to become abstinent and failed, I dived into despair. Margaret only replied, "I'm still proud of you. You have three days of healthy attitudes and normal eating."

As I accepted this gentleness, I trusted Margaret and the others in the support group. I quit masquerading as Kathleen, the sweat clothes frump, and began sharing my feelings, digging through them for the truth, and giving them back to God. I began a continuing abstinence that helped me quiet those condemning voices in my mind.

BRENDA, HUNGRY FOR APPROVAL

I felt demeaned standing before the doctor in that backless white gown. It was obvious my fourteen-year-old frame was not budding into the designated shape of a charming young lady.

"You know you're overweight, don't you?" the doctor said, and he gave me a diet plan. My mother looked at the floor—she must have felt humiliated, too. She was also overweight, and I was her pride and joy. I got decent grades in school; I was the only teenager who was asked to work in the church nursery; I helped Mom out at home with the cooking and cleaning. People used to say, "Brenda has such a cute face and a bubbly personality. If she'd only lose a little weight . . . ."

I attacked the diet, making sure Mom bought the food I needed. I still made popcorn for my little brothers, but I didn't put butter on a special bowl of popcorn for me. I eventually lost the extra pounds that summer. Even my dad, who drank a lot and barely noticed anything, commented on how cute I looked.

Then, when school started, boys started noticing me. I mentioned this to my mother, and she seemed troubled. No wonder—relationships with men weren't her strong point. My father never noticed her, even though she did everything he asked. Yet I liked being noticed by boys, especially by Seth, a basketball player. He began walking me home when he didn't have practice.

However, Seth was only a normal fourteen-year-old. He soon became interested in another girl, and I felt like nothing. I remember standing in front of the candy machine in the cafeteria after school. I didn't want to go home and cook and clean and do my homework, so I bought a candy bar and started to eat it.

"There's Brenda, at the candy machine," I heard a girl whisper.

"I wonder if she'll get fat again," snickered another.

I ran off with the candy bar and cried. After that, I kept up my decent grades and my responsible roles at church and home, but I ate like crazy.

I decided it didn't matter that I was overweight, because I did have some good friends, and they were overweight, too. In junior college, a smart, quiet guy noticed me and began calling me. He seemed intelligent, and I wanted to get married—I couldn't stay with my mom forever. Besides, I wanted to raise a family.

After I got married, I gained even more weight. I ate bedtime snacks to numb me out so I wouldn't be receptive to my husband's advances. Sometimes my lack of interest inflamed the quiet rage he carried inside him, but I didn't care because I had three beautiful children that I loved. I protected them from their father's coldness, and I gave them everything they needed. I helped out at a day-care center and eventually became the assistant director. I couldn't move up until I got a credential, but I didn't have enough confidence to go back to school.

Besides, I knew they wouldn't promote an overweight person like me. I tried dieting a few times, and I was miserable. I decided I'd rather be fat and happy.

When my older son started skipping school and taking drugs, I blamed it on my husband and his coldness, but when my daughter followed the same path, I panicked. What was wrong? Hadn't I created the perfect world for them? Why weren't they as loyal to me as I had been to my mother?

I felt so defeated that I ate even more. I found myself doing gross things like licking spilled ice cream off the freezer door. Once my daughter caught me picking food out of the garbage. I fired back at her in anger. That's when I called a woman who attended Overeaters Anonymous meetings. I went with her during the day so no one in my family would know.

A lot of people there weren't as heavy as I was, and I didn't like that. But they thought about food just the way I did. I could tell it was the most important thing in their lives. I heard them talk about getting well, even though their marriages were breaking up and their kids were running away.

I wanted the people in the group to like me, so I tried to impress them—I was funny one week, mature the next, pathetic the next. I felt uncomfortable, but I kept coming back. One day, my husband called me from work and told me I was lazy—me, the hard worker. I flew off to the OA meeting and dumped all my anger. Wow! Everyone talked to me afterward! Honesty had never helped me win friends before. After that, I tried to be more real, and I began reading the literature. I eventually got a sponsor, a woman who was doggedly determined that I didn't have to please her. Every time I'd ask, "Am I doing OK?" she would reply, "You're doing fine. It's progress, not perfection."

I discovered that I had my own thoughts and feelings that weren't so dumb after all. My family is very uncomfortable with my new self-respect. I believe that God loves me the way I am, so I don't pretend to be "little miss Christian" to try to get him to love me. I've lost some weight, and I'm still not slender, but I respect myself. I can now admit when I'm wrong, but I don't have to take the blame when I'm not. I see the changes in myself mirrored in the way my younger son talks to me. He is the only person in my family who treats me with respect, but that's today.

I'm still losing weight (very slowly), I'm still looking at my character defects, and I'm still allowing myself to grow.

FOOD: THE CENTER OF MY LIFE

Nancy, Kathy, and Brenda would now identify themselves as compulsive eaters. There's no predictable mold for those of us who wear this label. Some compulsive overeaters are named Chuck, Grant, and Ron, and they're stockbrokers and machine operators.

Some of us who are compulsive overeaters don't even look overweight. We aren't typically lazy, and very few of us are fat and jolly. We have one thing in common, however: We all use food to manage the pain in our lives. That feeling of a full stomach numbs our hurt and anger. Food is our major source of comfort, celebration, and companionship. Some people eat to sustain life; we eat to face life. We eat because of what is eating us.

Eating "nourishes" us, so to speak, because it becomes a substitute for tenderness, affection, excitement, and even sexual fulfillment. We may feel that life owes us those things, but since we're sure we aren't going to find them, food makes up for them. Food becomes our best friend, and without realizing it, we build our lives around it.

As our compulsion progresses, our willpower disintegrates. We eat when we're not hungry. We eat in secret, not wanting others to see how much we've eaten. We make excuses for why we have to eat—I have a headache, I feel nauseous. While others eat to live, we live to eat. We become disgusted with ourselves, and food becomes not only our best friend but also our worst enemy. Many of us become compulsive dieters, as controlling our weight becomes a driving force in our lives. It dominates our conversations, our choice of reading material, and our choice of friends. We can't live with food, but we can't live without it, either.

Only a compulsive eater . . .

- misses part of a conversation at a party because the chips and dip were just served
- licks a bowl of brownie batter so clean that another person can hardly tell if it needs washing
- wonders: When will I ever be at peace with food?

TWO

When Eating Takes Over

Is every overweight person a compulsive overeater? When does someone cross the line from eating a little too much to being a compulsive overeater?

We can't answer these questions for others because outward behaviors tell us little. Inner drives are the key, and only we can identify those for ourselves, and then only by being honest with ourselves.

There are some people who eat for comfort now and then, and it never progresses beyond that. We compulsive eaters usually begin overeating at a young age to face difficult situations. As adults we manage that reservoir of unresolved inner pain with food. Overeating becomes our primary coping mechanism. For example, when my spouse criticizes me, I may "need" a hot fudge sundae to feel better. If I don't like the way my mother talks to me, scarfing down a bag of potato chips helps. If I forget an important part of my presentation at work, I may soothe my embarrassment by hiding in my apartment this weekend and ordering in pizza as often as I like. We may not realize for a long time that we're using our old friend food to rescue us whenever we feel uncomfortable.

Gradually we begin to use eating to fill our emptiness in other ways. It becomes a companion to celebrate with in happy moments and a stimulant when life gets boring. We crown food our best friend.

As alcohol is to the alcoholic, food becomes our "drug of choice." At this point, compulsive eating isn't always a matter of how many ounces of food we eat or even the reasons we eat as much as the drivenness with which we eat. It's no longer just a mealtime or even a snack-time problem; it is a moment-by-moment obsession.

I can now admit that in my compulsive overeating days there were times when I felt that I wanted a certain food more than I wanted life itself. I ate off and on all day or thought about food all day, yet I didn't think I had a problem.

Eventually we see that using food to solve problems is like using airplane glue to repair the Concorde, but we keep using it anyway. "My overeating is like an anesthetic," says Linda. "It's as if I know I have a tumor, so I prepare for surgery, but then I cancel the painful surgery and simply take the anesthetic. Once it wears off, the pain is worse, and the tumor keeps growing."

By this time, our craving for food taints our entire lives. Psychiatrist Gerald May says in his book *Addiction and Grace* that addiction oppresses our desires, erodes our wills, confounds our motivations, and contaminates our judgment.[1]

DIETS CAN BE FATTENING

If compulsive eating is self-will gone berserk, compulsive dieting is self-control gone berserk. We compulsive dieters are encyclopedic in our knowledge of diets, fat grams, nutritional know-how, and exercise routines. We know the calorie count for most foods, and we know which restaurant in town sells "lite apple pie." We've read several of the two hundred diet books on the market; we've joined spas and tried diet clinics. We've tried hypnosis, diet pills, health resorts, and subliminal tapes.

We compulsive dieters are yo-yo dieters. I gained and lost the same fifteen pounds annually for twelve years. I tried every fad diet. I've weighed myself many times a day to see if a quarter of a pound had slipped away. I wore out several pairs of scales and dreamed of buying the kind my doctor used so I would always know how "bad" I was.

With each new diet, we think, *This one will do it,* as if it were a magical solution. We think that losing weight will suddenly enable us to cope with life and that people will automatically like us more.

There are some compulsive dieters who don't know much about nutrition. They may even think in extremes and make unrealistic goals, denying themselves any "bad" foods such as potatoes or carbohydrates. If exercising three times a week for thirty minutes is good, then exercising seven times a week for three hours is wonderful. This thinking is typical of compulsive eaters, who may eventually become bulimic (practicing binging and purging) or anorexic (practicing self-starvation).

Those of us who dedicate our energies toward losing weight the old-fashioned way, by dieting, eventually find that it doesn't seem to work anymore. It gets too difficult, our average weight creeps upward, and our self-loathing mushrooms. We, who prided ourselves in being able to lose weight, can no longer look ourselves in the eye in dressing room mirrors.

SYMPTOMS OF COMPULSIVE OVEREATING

Compulsive eating is characterized by five generally recognized addictive behaviors: tolerance, withdrawal symptoms, self-deception, loss of willpower, and distorted attention.[2]

> Tolerance: Do you need more food, more eating experiences or better ones to feel good?

At first, it takes just a little overeating to satiate the appetite. However, as our inner emptiness grows, it takes more food to satisfy us, and we develop cravings. We must eat more of our favorite foods more often. Finally, eating becomes the first thing we think about when we wake up and the last thing we think about as we drift off to sleep.

My own love affair with food began when I was a teenager and I drank a lot of soda pop. Then I began eating sandwiches before bedtime, and then I started eating chocolate and candy bars between meals. At the height of my compulsion, I was eating all day, stopping at convenience stores for snacks.

We can also tolerate more guilt. At first, we feel guilty for overeating, but we eventually learn to make excuses. Finally, it seems normal to be consumed by food instead of consuming it.

> Withdrawal symptoms: Do you get headaches, feel nauseous, or feel just plain unbearable when you don't get to eat as you had planned?

When food is withheld for some reason (perhaps our companion doesn't want to eat or it's inconvenient to stop), we feel agitated and grouchy and nothing seems right. We may experience mood swings—almost personality changes, depending on the availability of food. We can be happy one moment ("Stop—here's a place to eat!") and angry the next ("It's closed!"). Instead of being the people pleasers we know how to be, we show our "king baby" side, which demands things as if we're royalty in babyish, immature ways. We may try to hide these mood swings because they're so embarrassing. When food is withheld, we may even develop physical symptoms of ulcers and hypertension.

Even planned withdrawals, usually called "diets," become impossible. Dieting days are filled with tears, depression, irritability, or anger.

> Self-deception: Do you make excuses about why you eat or why you can't lose weight or why being overweight isn't a problem?

Denial is the recovery term for pretending a problem doesn't exist. We may say, "I'm not overweight, I'm just big-boned," or, "I can solve this overeating any time I want." When we look in the mirror, we may not even see the excess weight.

We may also deceive ourselves by blaming others for our problem: "I wouldn't eat so much except that my spouse does," or "I have to keep food around for my kids." They may prefer cheese curls to taco chips, but we continue buying taco chips because we like them—but we lie and say they're for the kids.

We move from deceiving ourselves to deceiving others. Fearing that others will discover our problem, we hide a stash of food or bury candy wrappers under the other garbage in the trash can. We eat before meeting a client for lunch at a restaurant so we won't have to eat so much in front of the client.

> Loss of willpower: Do you promise yourself you'll quit overeating, but you don't?

Even though it is technically possible for us to stop overeating, we feel as if we can't stop because our despair is so deep. While others give in to food temptations now and then, we face intense tugs-of-war several times a day. We wear down after so many battles, and after a while, eating normally seems impossible.

Well-meaning people ask, "Why don't you just stop overeating? Exercise some self-control." They don't understand the nature of addiction. We have programmed ourselves for years to manage our pain with overeating, and it's a betrayal of our compulsive bodies, hearts, and minds to change. It seems impossible to reprogram years of negative tapes that have played untruths in our minds.

Especially for those who profess a strong belief in God, the lack of control is baffling. Don't I have any willpower? We joke that "the spirit is willing, but the flesh is weak," but then we wonder in horror how we became so weak.

> Distorted attention: Do you find yourself unable to focus on your work or remember details about family activities because your mind is obsessed with eating?

Many times I nearly wrecked my car unwrapping a cheeseburger. Other times I fantasized about food so much that I didn't hear what others were saying. Once during a Bible study at my house, someone mentioned spaghetti for some reason. I began thinking about how I wanted to fix spaghetti after everyone left. As the others dug out eternal truths from the Bible, I planned how I would spice up the beef to taste like sausage. I was so focused on what the food would taste like, how it would look and how much I would enjoy it, that I missed anything God might have been trying to say to me through the Bible study. If he wanted me to befriend someone after the study, forget it. I was shooing everyone out the door so I could cook!

THE ADDICTIVE CYCLE

Another clue that our eating has become compulsive is if it follows certain before-and-after patterns. These patterns are called the *addictive cycle:* preoccupation, ritualization, compulsive eating, and despair. This cycle is generally recognized within the recovery movement as the pattern for addictive behaviors, and it was made even more popular by psychologist Dr. Patrick Carnes, designer and consultant to the sexual dependency unit of Del Amo Hospital in Torrance, California, in his book on sexual addiction, *Out of the Shadows.*[3]

Preoccupation: when the mind dwells obsessively on food, favorite foods, or eating experiences.

As compulsive eaters, we have a thought life different from that of others. We start looking forward to lunch at midmorning; after lunch, we start thinking about our midafternoon break; after that, we focus on dinner; and yes, after dinner, we root around for snacks.

We swing from eating opportunity to eating opportunity like a trapeze artist swings from one trapeze bar to another. Just as the trapeze artist can't afford to miss grabbing hold of that trapeze bar, we can't afford to miss an opportunity to eat, because we live for each one. To miss one means to die—at least emotionally.

Parties, celebrations, and holiday get-togethers mean food and food preparation to us. I used to anticipate church potlucks weeks in advance because of the variety of food, especially desserts. To eat so many desserts at once—wasn't that heaven?

Ritualization: routines that we follow before indulging in compulsive overeating.

Sarah passes three doughnut shops driving from her house to work. Her ritual is that she shows some supposed willpower by never stopping at the first shop; when she comes to the second shop, she stops if she's having a bad day; if it's a good day, she makes it to the third shop before she stops—but she always stops.

When she first began this ritual, Sarah circled the shop several times to give herself a chance to keep from going in. Now she circles the shop in a predatory way, as if she's claiming the territory for herself and announcing, "This is my turf."

We're as hooked on the rituals as we are on the eating. Going out to lunch is an emotional payoff for us. Having midnight snacks creates a full, satisfied feeling so we can sleep. Buying a chocolate bar at the end of an exhausting shopping trip is our reward. If we don't have a second or third helping at the table, we feel as if we've been cheated.

Rituals often include eating specific favorite foods, even certain name brands. They must be prepared exactly the way we like them. I remember that I was careful to spread a certain brand of mayonnaise on my sandwiches out to the corners of the bread. I went to great lengths to make the sandwiches just the way I wanted them.

> Compulsive eating: when a behavior or feeling triggers us into unplanned eating or into eating much more than we planned.

As our eating rituals develop, it doesn't take much to trigger the actual binge. A friend's inattentiveness sends us over to the snack table at a party for a finger full of chip dip when no one is looking. Then we cast appearances aside and fill our plate with chips and dip—several times.

Anger often triggers our compulsive eating. We use eating to get even with an employer, a parent, or a spouse. Munching on crunchy snack foods simulates the grinding of our teeth in anger. After all, we reason, isn't it better to relieve tension by overeating than snapping at my child or pulling out a gun?

When we feel helpless to defend ourselves, when we feel manipulated, when we've felt forced to comply, we turn to our best friend, food, to make it up to us. Gliding our tongue over those creamy foods soothes our irritations.

For ten seconds, life is wonderful. We feel good, our taste buds are satiated, and we feel temporarily relieved and peaceful.

> Despair: realizing that the overeating episode didn't solve anything.

It begins with a subtle disappointment—the kind you feel when you're troubled and you call a best friend but he or she doesn't have time for you. Then it deepens. You feel cheated and hopeless, the way you would feel if you spent a lot of money on a sports car only to find that its performance was nothing like what was promised. You begin wondering, *Is there anyone or anything that can help me?*

Thundering behind the disillusionment is a trainload of guilt. We tell ourselves, *This was a mistake. I shouldn't have eaten this much.* Then we use that mistake to thrash our character. We "beat ourselves up" by replaying negative tapes from the past such as *I'm a failure, I'll never be good enough.*

Self-loathing swallows us up, and we may even call ourselves names—"You fat freak!"—or smack ourselves or tear out our hair. We would never treat someone else this harshly, but we do it to ourselves with great ease.

Part of this guilt is healthy guilt because we have violated our conscience, which we gagged during the first three steps of the cycle. However, we poison this healthy guilt by using it excessively and by attacking who we are. We heap shame on ourselves, thereby breeding a venomous self-hatred.

The Next Step

The shame becomes so great that we need to escape from it, so we "numb out" by becoming preoccupied with food. Since preoccupation is the first stage of the cycle, the cycle repeats itself until it takes over our lives, and the guilt becomes more toxic each time.

FOUR CORE BELIEFS

The last step, despair, so rooted in shame, comes from the way we view ourselves and what we believe about ourselves. In his book *Out of the Shadows,*[4] Dr. Carnes lists four core beliefs that sex addicts have. I asked him in an interview if these applied to other compulsions as well, and he replied, "What I hear from most people is that the addictive system is familiar across the addictions. The first three of the core beliefs are common. What is unique to each addict is what you believe or trust that will meet your needs [the fourth belief]."

Here are the four faulty beliefs that Dr. Carnes says must be dealt with to break the cycle of addiction.

I'm Basically a Bad, Unworthy Person

At times we feel so inadequate that we believe we're not worthy of other people's love. It's not unusual to hear compulsive overeaters call themselves names or speak of themselves as criminals.

Our growing-up years may have taught us this belief. Says Carrie, "If I got five As and one B, my father asked me why I got the B. If I washed dishes, he'd find a spot and say, 'Do all these dishes over and do them right.' If something was missing, he'd line us kids up, cross-examine us, and accuse us of lying. Then, when he found whatever he'd misplaced, he'd laugh it off without apologizing. I'm sure he didn't mean to be so hard on us, but I felt that no matter how hard I tried, I'd never please him." Carrie took that childhood experience and magnified it many times until it reflected the way she viewed herself.

No One Would Love Me as I Am

It follows that if I believe I'm such a bad person, then I must hide my true self if anyone is going to like me. As we become more secretive about our compulsion, we feel we are so unlovable that we have to avoid intimacy, yet in public, we display a pseudo-confident image to get by.

When Mike, who is a pastor, preaches particularly stirring sermons, church members thank him sincerely. Mike never believes them, though. "Nobody's praise means anything to me," Mike told a support group. "I can't let it sink in because they're just seeing the part of me I can stand to show them. Someday, I'm going to get in the pulpit and say, 'I feel inadequate all the time; I love food more than I love God.' Can you imagine what people will think?" Many of us hide behind a "looking-good kid" facade. We try hard to appear good so others will like us. We're not being insincere, exactly, because we're trying to fool ourselves as much as anyone else. As a Christian, I did my best to walk the walk and talk the talk, but I knew I was failing miserably. I felt people would have been shocked if they knew me as I really was or knew how I much I loathed myself.

My Needs Are Never Going to Be Met If I Have to Depend on Others

Dr. Carnes notes that since addicts have been significantly disappointed by others, they don't depend on anyone. Since we don't trust people, we become fiercely determined to lick our own wounds without help from anyone else. It seemed to me that whenever I asked for help, it was more trouble than it was worth. Nothing a counselor or friend said seemed to help, so I felt abandoned. *Why did I even try to get help?* I would wonder. Gradually we prefer isolation—then we know to expect loneliness.

These feelings ruled the way I interacted in the first support group I attended. I excluded myself from the group for many weeks. When others talked about their problems, I felt empathy for them, but I backed away and ran out the door after the meetings while the others hugged and talked.

Food (or Spending or Sex) Is My Most Important Need

With all the ugliness of the above three beliefs, eating becomes our method of survival. Our deflated self-esteem is propped up with one more piece of fudge or a fifth piece of pizza. We create a fantasy world that says that if we get enough food, life will be wonderful.

We don't care if overeating affects our health, relationships, or ability to make a living; we've become slaves to it. Eating even becomes a substitute for God. We say we've given God our lives, but we hold back that most treasured thing—our compulsion. That's our secret place, where we can retreat when nothing else, not even God, works for us.

The first time I heard these core beliefs, I thought, *Not me. I'm such a nice girl.* But as I monitored my thoughts during the next week, I found they wore the many masks of these core beliefs. I saw how they played hide-and-seek with my positive motives and attitudes and that I needed the omnipresent Spirit to show me just how dysfunctional my thinking had become.

You May Be Wondering . . .

Q How can I figure out if I'm a compulsive overeater or simply someone who eats a lot?

A Compulsive overeaters are driven to eat and experience the symptoms of an addiction described above. Here's a quiz that OA uses:

Are You a Compulsive Overeater[5]

	Yes	*No*
1. Do you eat when you're not hungry?	_______	_______
2. Do you go on eating binges for no apparent reason?	_______	_______
3. Do you have feelings of guilt and remorse after overeating?	_______	_______
4. Do you give too much time and thought to food?	_______	_______
5. Do you look forward with pleasure and anticipation to the moments when you can eat alone?	_______	_______
6. Do you plan these secret binges ahead of time?	_______	_______
7. Do you eat sensibly before others and make up for it alone?	_______	_______
8. Is your weight affecting the way you live your life?	_______	_______
9. Have you tried to diet for a week (or longer) only to fall short of your goal?	_______	_______
10. Do you resent others telling you to "use a little willpower" to stop overeating?	_______	_______

	Yes	*No*
11. Despite evidence to the contrary, have you continued to assert that you can diet "on your own" whenever you wish?	_______	_______
12. Do you crave to eat at a definite time, day or night, other than mealtime?	_______	_______
13. Do you eat to escape from worries or trouble?	_______	_______
14. Have you ever been treated for obesity or a food-related condition?	_______	_______
15. Does your eating behavior make you or others unhappy?	_______	_______

The series of above questions may help you determine if you are a compulsive overeater. OA members find they have answered yes to many of these questions.

Q I never engage in binge eating (like gobbling six doughnuts or a box of Bugles). Is it still possible that I'm a compulsive eater?

A Many compulsive eaters do not binge. Compulsive eating is not about how much food we consume or the way in which we consume it. It's an emotional dependence on food. We use it to cope with life. Many compulsive eaters are even nutrition-conscious, picky eaters. Another reason many do not binge is that they're not only hooked on food but also fear it. They are hooked on controlling it, so they may stop eating long before they finish the bag of snack foods.

Recognize also that some binges occur in slow motion. We may not gobble a bag of chips all at once but instead may pinch it little by little over a few days. Others would forget it's on the shelf, but that's difficult for us to do.

Q What is the difference between an addiction and a compulsion?

A In the past, the word *addiction* was used to describe dependencies on things such as drugs and alcohol that affected the body chemically. Compulsions were thought to be behavioral only. Now we know that choices we make over and over about certain behaviors form a chemical path on the neurotransmitters in our brain. These paths make it likely that we'll repeat the behavior. Technically speaking, compulsive choices are chemical, too, and the distinction is gone. Even if this distinction were still common, food could be considered an addiction when it chemically affects the body in extreme ways, as sugar and caffeine often do. The distinction is now unclear and perhaps unnecessary, so I will use *addiction* and *compulsion* interchangeably in relation to compulsive eating.

THREE

What About My Faith?

We've examined how our compulsive eating follows its destructive cycle, and we've penetrated the deeper layer of our core beliefs. There's still another layer of ourselves that must be examined: the spiritual.

Some argue that compulsive overeating is not a spiritual issue but only a nutritional or psychological one, or perhaps both. No doubt you've encountered these approaches:

> Limited nutritional and medical approach: If I just knew more about fat grams or could check myself into a treatment center, I could lose weight.

People keep telling us that our overeating behaviors can be modified by using rewards and punishments or by simply knowing more about how we metabolize food, yet most of us have tried some version of this approach and failed.

> Limited psychological approach: If I could work out my anger from the past, I would eat less.

Learning new ways to cope and resolving pain from the past speak to the reasons we eat, but we must also address the deepest parts of ourselves, where we decide who we are and why we are alive. Until we properly align our spiritual roots, we're only putting masking tape over a gunshot wound and hoping the bullet lodged in our body won't do any harm.

COMPULSIVE EATING IS A SPIRITUAL ISSUE

As we progress in our compulsive eating, we try to pull out of food what we can only get from God.

Food Is a Thing to Be Worshipped

We worship food as we fantasize about the sight, touch, and taste of food. We long for it in our hearts. We give a lot of time to being preoccupied with it, following our eating rituals, and feeling guilty about overeating. Our compulsive overeating becomes a source of power as we use it to control, shape, and fix our world. We center our lives around it, which makes it our god.

Food Is Love

The basic problem, which I've heard over and over in support groups, is that we don't believe that God loves us. We want to know that we are special enough that someone will love us no matter what. We may have tried to acquire that love from people, and they may have offered as much as they were able, but their love was not adequate. Therefore, we tried to find love in our eating experiences.

Food Is Identity

In the broadest sense, spiritual issues are those that define who we are, and we have defined ourselves as people who rely on food. Said licensed family and addiction counselor Father Peter Canavan, S.A., "Addiction involves spiritual problems because it is created out of lack of relationships with self. The addiction stands in the vacuum of the person."[1]

You may think, *Food doesn't mean that much to me,* and perhaps it doesn't. Only as I entered recovery did I see how cleverly food had become woven into and out of the fibers of who I was. Only in recovery did I monitor myself and discover that my moment-to-moment thoughts, even my jokes, centered on overeating. Only in recovery did Starla admit, "I feel as if I've been in a coma for years. Now that I'm not chasing food, I'm seeing and hearing my children for the first time in my life. I love to sit and watch them now—they do such cute things! Where was I all those years?"

Our overeating is also a spiritual issue because it thrashes our relationship with God. After counseling many addicted priests, psychologist Dr. Louis Stoetzer of the Adult Children's Center in Orange, California, concludes, "Anyone who has an addiction also has a very poor relationship with God. Their prayer life is one of desperation and pleading. They use lots of global requests—please make me feel better, please make me stop doing this. Their relationship with God is colored by the shame and guilt of addiction. They feel distant from God because they feel either that God doesn't care or that he can't help them."[2]

It seems as if God doesn't care because even if we prayed about our diets, they failed, or when we did lose weight, we gained it back, just as 95 percent of Americans do.[3] After a while, a shadowy feeling develops within us that God isn't doing everything he could to help us. Between that and other disappointments in life, we may have even become mad at God.

Mad at God? Many compulsive eaters entering recovery feel mad at God, though most find it difficult to admit it. Others will say they're frustrated with God because he doesn't seem to be listening. Our compulsive eating drives us so hard that we cry out to God for help, but nothing seems to happen.

Our frustration and anger with God show themselves in the way that we quit going to church, quit reading the Bible, and quit praying. We may even try to alienate church members or people we consider spiritual leaders.

In retrospect, I can say that I was mad at God and burned out with spiritual things. My anger showed itself not so much in railing but in a weariness toward God. What prayers I prayed were mechanical. I went to church as little as possible, which is interesting for a pastor's wife to try! I detached myself from almost everything that was spiritual. My compulsive eating, spending, and raging needed more room in my life, and I gave to them the room I used to give God. I felt as if I were held hostage by these feelings, and I didn't believe that God would ever rescue me. At times, it was as if he and I were no longer on speaking terms.

Our compulsive behavior is intertwined with our limited spirituality. This means that if you're working on your recovery, expect to find spiritual issues confronting you—for example, Where is God? Why won't he help me? And, if you're a compulsive eater who seeks God, expect him to confront you about your compulsions. God wants to be Lord of our lives. He won't play second fiddle to cheesecake or filet mignon.

LIMITED SPIRITUAL UNDERSTANDING

Why do so many compulsive overeaters who espouse a faith in God feel they have "tried" God but found him wanting? A recovering therapist notes in OA literature: "[The program] doesn't work easily for those who . . . have had *religion so overemphasized* in their upbringing that the spiritual aspects of the program trigger what amounts to an allergic attack."[4] I would clarify that statement to say it is not religion per se but a limited form of religion that overemphasizes works and deemphasizes God's grace. This limited understanding poisons us because it perpetuates our compulsive eating rather than helping us face it.

Some of these limited ideas are wrong, others are good ones gone wrong, and still others are good ones that lack sufficient depth. Here are a few to consider.

"Guilt and Shame Keep Me Good"

The guilt is heavy for Christians who are compulsive eaters. We know we are abusing our bodies, the temples of the Holy Spirit (1 Cor. 6:19). We feel like criminals who have been caught—we're exposed, tied up, and unable to move. We feel isolated, as if everyone knows our problem and feels disgusted with us. We lecture ourselves with Scripture, hoping that a self-scolding will do the trick.

"I thought that God would take away my binging if I prayed more or helped people more, so I did those things," says Gwen. "I volunteered my summers in missionary service so I could help others. I even went to starving countries, hoping that it would shame me out of binging. It didn't work."

We're terrified of what will happen if we stop dieting and stop feeling guilty. We think that if we just feel guilty enough, we'll stop overeating, so we grind ourselves hard through the guilt phase of the addictive cycle.

Shame not only doesn't work but also fuels our compulsive eating. It shoves us into the addictive cycle as we become even more preoccupied with overeating. This "guilt is good" mentality highlights our faltering steps and cripples us even more. Says Jeannie, "For years I beat myself up for eating too much, and it made me more compulsive. I started drinking, and then I looked for acceptance in relationships with men. It wasn't until I became secure in the love of my support group members and finally in God's love that I quit condemning myself and stopped drinking and overeating."

"The most important thing that addicted persons need to do," says psychologist Dr. Patrick Carnes, "is reduce the shame. It's like the shame of a little child who realizes that he can't do what other little kids do and says, 'What's wrong with me that I'm different?' As adults, the shame is exponential because they wonder, Why is it that other people can eat normally and I can't? So they feel bad about themselves."[5]

But aren't we, in fact, guilty?

There is a difference between healthy guilt and unhealthy guilt. Healthy guilt helps us see that we have violated the rights of others, and it leads us to want to make amends. It acknowledges wrongdoing but affirms that we are still redeemed children of God. God doesn't have to love everything we do in order to love us.

Unhealthy guilt, or shame, immobilizes us and keeps us from changing. We believe we are ultimately bad people doomed to keep stumbling through life the same way.

"I Must Be a 'Looking-Good Kid'"

When I led an eating disorders group at my church, I knew what to expect when church friends found out I was involved in the group. They stared, they cringed, they asked, "You'll be where Tuesday night?" I'd always tried so hard to be a "looking-good kid" that in my recovery I found it freeing to admit to people that I was a compulsive overeater.

Just as Christians often dress up to go to church, too many of us dress up in pseudo peace and cheerfulness to cover up our ragged feelings of anger and fear. Part of being a Christian, supposedly, is being a "together person."

Even worse, we confuse our pseudo image of ourselves with who we are. We think that if we pretend to be normal eaters and problem solvers, then we are those things. Disillusionment sets in as soon as we come home from church, wolf down a double-size lunch, yell at our kids, and refuse to face our relationship problems.

Our perfectionism and "looking-good" images are cover-ups for shame. We feel so inadequate that we have to try to prove ourselves to ourselves, to each other, and even to God. We feel compelled to be Supermom, Superorganizer, Superachiever just to disprove our deep feelings of low self-esteem.

All this frantic effort is, of course, counter to Christianity, which tells us that God is the one who makes us good enough. The truth is that "the Christian church is the only society in the world in which membership is based upon the qualification that the candidate shall be unworthy of membership."[6]

"God Is Ashamed of Me When I'm Not Perfect"

How do you feel about these statements?

- God would love me even if I weighed three hundred pounds.
- God loves me when I lean into the refrigerator and eat everything in sight.

- God loves me even as I stand in front of a full-length mirror naked and hate what I see.

We compulsives typically have a shaming view of God. We assume that God condemns us the way we've repeatedly condemned ourselves, which multiplies our shame. We're certain that he abhors us in our compulsive eating. We see him as a cosmic security guard waiting to zap us for our sins or as a distant sleeping giant who began ignoring us long ago. Women and men who have been physically or sexually abused by their parents may distrust any parent figure, including God.

All these condemning, shaming views of God fuel our compulsive overeating because they rob us of a Safe Person we need to be loved by. We miss the truth: that God loves and even works through fallible, hurting people. He loved and worked through murderers such as Moses, King David, and the apostle Paul (a mass murderer!). Many other Bible heroes behaved so miserably that today's Christians would never allow them to be leaders in their church.

How have we missed seeing God as genuine and caring? Often, God's justice is emphasized to the exclusion of his mercy. The upshot is that we think that God doesn't love us when we sin, especially on days when our eating is out of control.

"If I Know What's Right, I'll Be Able to Do It"

Several times well-meaning leaders took me aside and asked me why the members of our eating disorders group didn't just stop eating.

"Give them Bible verses to memorize," one suggested. "Teach them about nutrition."

"We know lots of Bible verses," I explained. "Now we're trying to live them."

He still looked confused, so I asked him, "How many calories are there in an average piece of pumpkin pie?"

He didn't know.

"350," I replied.

"Which gym in town has the most equipment and offers the most exercise classes?"

He didn't know, so I told him.

"My problem isn't that I don't know the facts about nutrition, exercise, and weight gain," I explained. "My problem is that I'm paralyzed by them. Knowing the rules and being empowered to follow them are two different things."

Thinking that knowing facts is enough increases our compulsivity because we punish ourselves with knowledge, saying, *I should know better—what's wrong with me?*

"Knowing" things is never enough. I can recite the names of the Old Testament patriarchs, but my faith runs far short of these all-too-fallible men. I can recite the fruit of the Spirit in three seconds, but I'm not sure I've lived any of them well for even one day—but I'm progressing. True knowledge is a process that permeates our whole selves. Imagine that you have dropped a roll of paper towels onto the floor, where red punch has been spilled. In the first split second, the punch dampens the bottom towel only. After another second, the bottom half of the roll is soaked. In another second, the entire roll is drenched. Knowing that I shouldn't overeat is similar to the punch soaking the bottom towel only. I need to experience the truth through all the layers of myself.

My mind "knows" that overeating is harmful to my body, emotions, and spirit, but my body is used to being stuffed, and my emotions are used to being numbed. My spirit is used to looking for comfort in eating, not in God. It takes time to soak that roll of paper towels, and it takes months and years of recovery to reteach our bodies, our minds, our emotions, and our spirits.

"God Is Going to Heal Me"

"Why can't God just heal me?" Bonnie wailed. "I'm tired of trying to get better." Her struggle had been so long and so intense that I found myself echoing her question.

Then I remembered Joe. He'd given up his alcoholism and drug addiction in a treatment center. He prayed and asked God to relieve him of his desire to smoke. After three months, he stopped, and the desire to smoke completely left him. Now he battles the last monster: compulsive overeating. He's four years into his battle with this final addiction, and he has periods of abstinence and periods of indulgence. Yet it's been good. He has had to grow in his recovery in ways that his other addictions never demanded of him.

I have seen God miraculously and instantaneously relieve people of compulsive overeating, but not often. In Joe's case, it seems that God jump-started him through recovery by helping him with his more life-threatening addictions. Now God is helping him to work through this last difficult one. Joe continually looks back with gratefulness on his healing, and it gives him courage to battle his compulsive overeating.

When we plead with God to miraculously heal us of this craving, and he doesn't do as we ask, we may assume we aren't good enough or we don't have enough faith or that God doesn't love us. This gets us into trouble because we are assuming that God's will is that we be miraculously healed and that he does this for everyone.

We're also forgetting that it may be that a miraculous healing isn't as ultimately beneficial to the person being healed as the process of recovery. Being healed from a compulsion solves one problem only—the eating; recovery solves many problems. Recovery gives us a chance to work through our fear and anger and to add spiritual disciplines that we might otherwise never attempt to our lives.

What could be more miraculous than recovery—learning to solve problems, finding a new ability to love people, and developing a new capacity for knowing God? This kind of transformation is miraculous, even though it isn't instant, and it requires spiritual tools besides prayers of desperation. When you look at the result—a recovery of spirit—it is no less dramatic than an instantaneous healing. It's actually more dramatic, because you're not only forsaking a behavior but also finding new tools to live your life and a new perspective on God. This is much deeper than a healing of the behaviors or appetite.

Recovery takes too long, some complain. How fast I'm progressing is not the issue. I don't want my spiritual growth to be like the forced maturation of a hothouse tomato, yielding only a cardboard taste. If you rush, you become an imitation Christian with no real heart for God. I want my spiritual growth to be firm, full-flavored, and bright red.

You May Be Wondering . . .

Q As a Christian, I'm a new creation. Shouldn't my eating problem take care of itself?

A God promises there will be no sorrows in heaven, but he doesn't promise that about life on earth. Becoming a new creation in Christ means that I set my path in a new direction and that God empowers me on that path. It doesn't mean I become perfect. It's still a journey to seek God, just as the Israelites in the Old Testament journeyed to the Promised Land. They went through many trials (crossing the Red Sea, worshipping the idol at Mt. Sinai, wandering for forty years) before they even arrived at the Promised Land. Then they still had to take possession of it. The Christian life is a lifelong journey to "take possession of the land" (possessing the abundant life Christ promised), but we fight many battles and enjoy many victories along the way.

PART TWO

How Do I Get Better?

FOUR

What It Takes to Change

The therapist leading the workshop asked us to draw a picture of our eating disorder. I drew several tall pillars and supporting crossbeams of an empty house with no walls. It vaguely resembled the porch of an ancient Greek building. Its empty look scared me, so I pressed the lead of the pencil sideways against the page and filled the empty house with a mist. Immediately I sensed that the mist represented the eating that filled my life as a teenager and made me happy.

Where did that come from? I wondered. A few minutes before, the workshop leader had asked us when our eating disorder began, and I had reflected on my life as a shy, lonely teenager, the only child in the house. I had used food to bring excitement into what I perceived as a dreary existence.

As I stared at my drawing, I knew that the healthy thing to do was to erase the mist from the house, just as I was abstaining from compulsive overeating. Yet, even with two years of recovery at the time I attended the workshop, I found myself reluctant to erase it. The thought of giving up compulsive overeating forever still scared me. The potential emptiness of that house still scared me. How could I give up this thing that made the house (and my life) fun and interesting to live in? How would I survive in an empty house?

Then I began lightly doodling a cloud to absorb the mist. What was this cloud? I wondered. Immediately I thought of how I'd been praying, meditating, and reading the Psalms, activities that flowed out of my new search for God. My doodles were my way of saying that God's presence, his comfort, his liveliness were filling the emptiness inside me. I was a little bit more ready to betray my best friend, food, and surrender it to God.

It's interesting that the doodling, which was my way of calling on God's presence, kicked in so automatically. With two years of recovery, surrender was becoming an automatic response to fear.

What does it take to surrender our faithful companion—and our worst foe?

"HITTING BOTTOM"

In AA meetings, alcoholics talk about getting so low in life that they finally "hit bottom." Compulsive overeaters have to get desperate, too. We have to be disgusted at our drivenness to overeat. We have "to be sick and tired of being sick and tired," as they say in AA.

If you're just dissatisfied with being overweight, that's not enough. If you think you have one more surefire diet to try, you aren't ready. You must feel so much genuine despair that you are desperate. You must be so broken that you're willing to turn your back on your best friend, food.

It took me years to be willing to give up food. I visited an OA meeting for the first time many years ago. The people at the meeting had a serenity that impressed me, but they also scared me. I could see that they weren't just planning to lose a little weight—they were changing their entire attitude toward food. I didn't go back, because I knew I was too tightly bonded with food.

It wasn't until several years later, when I was desperate, that I considered attending another meeting. My husband had told me that he wanted to leave me because my critical nature had worn him to the bone. He wanted to take our kids with him so that I wouldn't wear them down with criticism, too.

My husband was right about me. If he left a bath towel lying around, I scolded: "You never clean up after yourself." If he vacuumed the living room, I complained that he didn't do it right and vacuumed it again.

I had taken on the role that alcoholics call "king baby" to describe themselves when they must have everything their way. The rest of the family tiptoes around this king baby family member so he or she won't get upset. This king baby must either control everybody's life or make their lives unpleasant. Somewhere within myself, I knew I was a "king baby," and I had been praying about my critical spirit for years. It seemed that this part of my nature would never die.

As a result of this marital crisis, I put myself on a forced march of kindness. That sounds inconsistent, and it was. How does a habitually critical person force herself to be kind? With great difficulty: by faking it all the time and by sheer terror of abandonment.

In the process of forcing myself to act kind, I became sick of myself, sick of the way I judged people, sick of the way I treated them like baggage. As I struggled to be more kind, I ranged from euphoric highs to disillusioned lows—and the lows got deeper and more frequent.

As a compulsive overeater, I knew only one way to cope with so much disillusionment, fear, and grief. I ate a lot and all the time. I could no longer diet, because dieting made me grouchy, and I had to be kind.

In the meantime, I confessed my critical spirit to God many times a day and asked for help. I made what I thought was a lot of progress, but it seemed like nothing to my husband. He and I both knew I was faking it.

That's when I "hit bottom" emotionally and admitted to God I had no idea how to be kind and caring. Whether my husband stayed or left, I did not like the person I'd become. Would you teach me to be kind? I asked God.

Finally, my will was broken. I no longer thought I knew everything. I wanted to change—not to please my husband but to please God and to be able to live with myself.

The pain and brokenness were so great I was exploding inside, and there was not enough food in the world to prevent those explosions. Finally, I visited OA meetings again and wound up in a church-related eating disorders support group, patterned after OA.

Soon this support group became the most important meeting in my life. It was the only place where I felt understood and where I could share my splintered feelings. Before my crisis, those kinds of meetings had been too scary to attend; in my crisis, life was so scary I had to attend them. I needed one safe place of honesty and love.

We all "hit bottom" in different ways. Some become desperate when their child or friend catches them binging. Others come to themselves when they've nearly lost custody of their kids. Still others have almost lost their jobs or come to financial ruin. The crisis can be large or small, obvious or subtle, but it must crack that "I'm too smart" veneer. It must force us to open our minds and make us willing to listen to ideas that we otherwise would have thought were too simple to work.

THE POWER OF GENUINE DESPERATION

Attempting recovery to please someone else doesn't work. I'm glad I didn't visit OA when I was only afraid of losing my husband because it wouldn't have fostered real recovery. True surrender has nothing to do with pleasing someone else or solving a crisis. You work your recovery because you are desperate to have God change your life. In my case, it wasn't my husband's confrontation that moved me into recovery, although it helped me see the truth about myself. As I faced how powerless I was to change, I became sick of myself. I admitted that it was more important to be kind to those I loved than to be a high-achieving person. I needed that inner nausea and brokenness to make me want to forsake compulsive eating.

Desperation was the missing ingredient for the person described in James 1:23–24: "Anyone who listens to the word but does not do what it says is like a man who looks at his face in a mirror, and after looking at himself, goes away and immediately forgets what he looks like." Desperation makes it impossible to forget what we look like in the mirror. Our brokenness is ever before us.

ADMITTING BROKENNESS

One day my recovery friend Debbie called and admitted eating half of a cheesecake, a sliver at a time. She was grieving over her and her husband's infertility problem.

Debbie talked for a while about their grief. Then, somewhat irritated, yet resigned, she said, "I know what you're going to say. You're going to tell me how you've had to keep surrendering things over and over: 'I can't, God can, I'll let him.'" (These are an abbreviated version of the first three Steps of the Twelve Steps.)

Surrender is the primary issue. With each problem in my life, the key is to turn it over to God:

- I'm powerless over food, over my appetite, over my spouse, over how our relationship grows, over my career, over my financial success.
- My power is limited. I have done everything I can do, and now it's God's business.
- I will never prove my self-worth by being good enough, achieving enough, working hard enough so I can be worth something.
- I surrender my grandiosity: What I believe is best in this situation may not be the best thing after all—I give up trying to have my own way.
- I will consider the suggestions of others, even if I'm sure their ideas are wrong or silly.

Clarity

As we turn ourselves over to God, we realize that what we thought was our treasure was actually our troublemaker. I had always feared giving up compulsive overeating because it would ruin my life; now I saw that compulsive overeating had already helped me ruin my life, and I feared that I would never give it up. This clarity frees us to move on.

Gratefulness

Brokenness brings a flood of grace into our lives, crowding out some of the bitterness. I felt grateful for OA instead of fearful of it. I thanked people for second chances instead of demanding them. I felt relieved that I could stop beating up on myself long enough to listen for God's voice.

Empowerment

We defuse the addictive cycle because we surrender each stage: When we're preoccupied with food, we give up our preoccupation; when we're practicing our rituals, we give them up; even when we feel guilty, we give that up, too.

Giving up works because it bypasses willpower, about which psychiatrist Dr. Gerald May says, "The fundamental mind trick of addiction is focusing attention on willpower."[1] Willpower no longer works for us because it is a powerful player in the preoccupation phase of the addictive cycle. It makes us even more preoccupied with overeating. Instead, we preoccupy ourselves with surrender and focus on our higher power, God. We admit our powerlessness, step aside, and let the Holy Spirit do his work: "For it is God who works in you to will and to act according to his good purpose" (Phil. 2:13).

THE CONTROL TRIP

Surrender can be particularly difficult for controllers and confirmed individualists. We are the kind of people who feel that we are usually right or that we can take care of matters ourselves. *Take your hands off, thank you,* is our response to overtures to help. We feel we need to break with others and move ahead. We believe we will find some new diet, health clinic, or behavior modification technique to overcome our weight problem.

The idea of turning things over to God, of letting go, of keeping things simple is alien to our individualistic can-do culture. We think we can do anything if we just roll up our sleeves, pull up our socks, and get going. Give us a little time, and we can control, shape, fix, and change anybody and anything. How humbling to find that we haven't controlled or fixed ourselves and that we won't.

My own control trip had grown out of straining to be good enough (virtuous) for God. I tried to find the right formulas to reshape myself into a better person. All that straining wore me out, discouraged me, and made me insensitive to others. Madeleine L'Engle gets at the heart of the problem in her book *Walking on Water: Reflections on Faith and Art.*

> We live under the illusion that if we can acquire complete control, we can understand God . . . But the only way we can brush against the hem of the Lord, or hope to be part of the creative process, is to have the courage, the faith, to abandon control.
>
> For the opposite of sin is faith and never virtue, and we live in a world which believes that self-control can make us virtuous. But that's not how it works. How many men and women we have encountered, of great personal virtue and moral rectitude, convinced of their own righteousness, who have been totally insensitive to the needs of others, and sometimes downright cruel![2]

It's been a struggle to understand that trying to be good enough doesn't work. I just have to love God and let him love me: "I delight greatly in the Lord; my soul rejoices in my God. For he has clothed me with garments of salvation and arrayed me in a robe of righteousness" (Isa. 61:10). God, the only good enough one, will make me righteous, not my own self-controlling efforts.

THE VICTIM TRIP

Sometimes we go to the opposite extreme and think we can't do anything about any of our problems. We play the victim role and live in regret, or we wish our life away, or we live through others and hide from life and its relationships. We've needed our compulsive overeating to victimize us so we have an excuse for not becoming the person God intended.

We need to surrender that role, which can be scary. We may be afraid of our buried feelings or afraid to make ourselves vulnerable. We become desperate when we're tired of being victims and watching everyone else play in the game of life while we look on.

The only thing that makes the risk worth it is that we know that God is in control. We can trust ourselves to listen for instructions and trust him to empower us to follow them. The Bible is full of "I can't" heroes. Gideon said he couldn't defeat the Midianites, and Moses said he couldn't lead the Israelites out of Egypt. What we don't realize is that God's power works best when we surrender. Then he wins battles with pocket-size armies (as he did with Gideon), and he parts Red Seas (as he did with Moses), and we stand there surprised. God's method is grace, which we experience as we give up our controlling roles and victim roles: "Grace seeks us but will not control us," writes Gerald May.

> Saint Augustine once said that God is always trying to give good things to us, but our hands are too full to receive them. If our hands are full, they are full of the things to which we are addicted. And not only our hands, but also our hearts, minds, and attention are clogged with addiction. . . . we can choose whether to relax our hands a little or to keep clenching them ever more tightly.[3]

We're so afraid to relax our grip on our roles and to give up. Jesus Christ's most broken moment, dying on the cross, was also a most powerful moment as God unleashed the power to redeem humans. Our surrender unleashes us from the past and gives us freedom to move on.

You May Be Wondering . . .

Q But isn't self-control a good thing?

A Yes, in its place. The problem is that we neglect the things we can control (what food is bought at the grocery store and whether or not we attend support group meetings) and try to control the things we can't (the feelings and actions of others, including God). We need to ask God's help to control those things that are within our power and completely surrender all those things beyond our power.

Q Doesn't being powerless leave me even more open to temptation?

A No. The admission of powerlessness is actually an admission of our humanity. Man has always tried to be like God, beginning in the garden of Eden. We're surrendering that greed to be more than human and choosing instead to find empowerment through God.

FIVE

Abstinence: A Tool, Not a Goal

On the end of my purse zipper is attached a metal rectangle about an inch long. I can't read it anymore because some of the letters of the well-known footprints reading are worn away. Now that this trinket is worn and battered, it is even more meaningful to me. It is the token my first support group used as a "chip" to recognize each of us for our first thirty consecutive days of abstinence from compulsive overeating.

What exactly is abstinence? It is abstaining from our compulsive eating behaviors, whatever they may be. These behaviors may include snacking, binging, snitching food as we prepare meals, or even gulping food down in a frenzied way. We may wish to include our rituals in the list of behaviors from which we abstain. There's no more driving home the long way so we can pass the ice cream parlor, no more buying snack foods supposedly for our family or roommate when they're actually for our "stash." Overeaters Anonymous wisely suggests that a person pick his or her own abstinence. (This is the topic of the next chapter.)

ABSTINENCE VERSUS DIETING

Abstinence is not a diet, and in many ways it is the opposite of a diet.

Permanent Versus Temporary

A diet is a short-term eating plan that lasts only a month or two, while abstinence lasts the rest of your life, one day at a time.

Dieting is a stopgap measure and can be compared to having surgery done for a continuing growth. That kind of surgery never cures us; it only eliminates the growth. Abstinence and recovery attack the cause of the growth and help the tissue repair itself.

Realism Versus Extremism

Compulsive overeating is an extreme form of eating, and so we often choose extreme dieting solutions, such as fasting or using liquid diets.

Abstinence gives us a peek at the real and normal world of eating. We still have to face the monster three times a day and make decisions about foods we love, not just about grapefruit and cottage cheese. We learn to cope in the thick of battle, when we're preparing food or ordering it at a restaurant: Will I put a lot of butter on this potato? Will I give in and order French fries? Abstinence prepares us to eventually live at peace with food in the real world.

Attitude Versus Behavior Only

Abstinence is a state of mind in which we want a healthy life free of a preoccupation with food. When I dieted, I was even more preoccupied with food as I measured and weighed each item. If I got hungry, I read yummy recipes in cookbooks, especially ones with beautiful colored pictures, in order to satisfy my appetite. I wasn't overeating, but my love affair with food continued and even grew.

In recovery, my attitude changed. In Los Angeles, there is a drive-in restaurant with a huge doughnut towering on top of it about forty feet high. It is situated next to the freeway on ramp I used almost daily. Early in my abstinence, I tried not to look at the doughnut when I passed it. About four months into my abstinence, I found myself staring directly at the huge brown doughnut, sticking out my tongue, and yelling, "No thanks, buster!"

That was my way of saying that even my heart would no longer be ruled by food. I was venting healthy anger at the control my compulsion had held over me. I was expressing my determination to choose peace and serenity instead.

Surrender Versus Control

Abstinence is an eating plan that we choose with God's help and that we recommit to him every day. We turn our need to eat over to God and ask him to help us. We hold no illusions that we alone have mastered compulsive eating, and that's important.

A diet is a form of control, which inflames addictive behavior because "it is in the very nature of addiction to feed on our attempts to master it," notes Gerald May.[1] That's why dieting doesn't help our compulsive eating; it inflames it. A diet is our attempt to repair ourselves, and self-repair does not work for us. We agree instead to report back to the factory to have the Master Designer refurbish our inner parts that have quit working.

DIFFERENCES BETWEEN RECOVERY AND ABSTINENCE

Recovery, as the word is used by Twelve-Step groups, refers to the process of learning to live a life of serenity in which we relinquish our compulsive behavior. We admit our powerlessness over that behavior and ask God to overcome it through us. In this process, we take responsibility for our faults and the wrongs we've done, and we practice making conscious contact with God.

Abstinence is not our goal, but it is an important tool of recovery. Abstinence helps us gain recovery because when we're not chasing after food and binging on sugar, we have more clarity to see life events for what they are.

It's not uncommon to meet people with abstinence but no recovery. They may still talk incessantly about food, calories, and weight loss, but they've never practiced Twelve-Step principles (most of which happen to be biblical ones).

I went on a trip with a woman named Connie who had an abstinence of sorts but no recovery. At every meal, she played with her food like most of my anorexic friends do. Also like them, she complained endlessly about how tasteless or fattening the food was. An hour before each meal, she began talking about how she hoped the meal wasn't going to be too high in calories. She finally skipped one meal.

In the mornings, she changed her clothes several times, matching her socks with her earrings. Did this look right? she asked us. I felt grieved by her neediness. She needed to be perfect. If a hair was out of place, she panicked. One of those mornings she explained to me, "You see, I used to be really heavy. Now that I've lost the weight, I'm very concerned about my appearance."

At the end of the retreat, she asked us to leave early so we could eat at a restaurant, so we did. Even though she ordered what she wanted, she complained about how fattening the food was and then set it aside. Her love-hate relationship with food was so familiar to me from my former compulsive days that I could see it was still ruling her. Technically, one could say that she was "abstinent," but this was not recovery. This was slavery.

This woman's lack of recovery reminds me of what I heard a wise recovering alcoholic say: "When you were drinking, your car was in reverse. Once you put the cork in the bottle, you've put your car into neutral. But only through recovery can you get your car into drive." Simple abstinence is putting the car in neutral. It takes a lot more than that to get yourself out on the road.

GENERAL GUIDELINES FOR ABSTINENCE

How Abstinence Works

One Day at a Time Our drive for control and perfectionism tells us to become abstinent and never overeat again. Reminding ourselves that we choose to be abstinent only for today relieves the pressure on the perfectionism valve. Like the Israelites who received their manna from God each day, we plan our food one day at a time, and one day is enough. More than a daily portion spoils.

There's a freedom in planning our food for the day and being done with it. We don't have to focus on food and wonder all day, *What will I have for dinner? What will I order at the restaurant?* Pondering these questions gets the preoccupation part of the addictive cycle going. It has helped me to plan menus ahead of time so I'm making my choices in calm moments when I'm not hungry. I avoid at all costs wandering the supermarket at 6:00 P.M. when I'm hungry.

Knowing that we've chosen to be abstinent for only one day, today, outwits our delinquent willpower. I used to pass a convenience store and postpone a binge, telling myself I'd chosen to be abstinent only today. There will be other days, and other convenience stores, I'd say. I no longer needed willpower because I was abstinent only for today.

This nondemanding, easy-does-it attitude is a practical application of God's grace. So many times when I feel hungry, I surrender the hunger to God, and within the next few minutes I have a mysterious sense of feeling full. I can't explain this except to say that when I surrender my hunger, God's grace rushes in.

Accountability Many of us have isolated ourselves because we've thought we could be loved only if we were perfect in every way. We may think a team approach is the last thing that would work, but in reality it's often the best. We can make ourselves accountable to a person or group whom we trust and whom we know will accept us even if we blow it. This may be a support group, a trusted friend, a therapist, or what Twelve-Step groups call a "sponsor." A sponsor is a partner who has more recovery than we have and who can support us and warn us if we're getting sidetracked. Some compulsive eaters make themselves accountable to food sponsors, partners whom they call every day to report their specific eating plan for that day. Being accountable for abstinence also means that we recommit it every day to God and that we will reach out to someone else in recovery for help if we're tempted to deviate from our chosen abstinence.

Counting Days It's good to count days of abstinence (I counted hours in the beginning!) because they gather momentum as we move through them. We share our success (and our failures, too) with our sponsor and our support group because this is a team effort.

We don't want to give in because it's too difficult to start again. We stay abstinent just for today, and then we have one more day to lean upon. We get on a roll, so to speak, and a seed of abstinence gives way to a stem, then to a blossom, then finally to an entire plant.

Choosing My Best Weight Another area of latitude that OA philosophy allows is that we may select what we believe is our normal weight. This "normal weight" may be different from the pencil-thin standard our culture promotes. Instead, we aim for the weight that gives us the most energy and that our body is comfortable maintaining. We seek God about choosing our goal weight. As we get closer to that weight, we may continue to seek him about refining our abstinence so that our goal weight is achievable.

Eating That's Nnnnnnnormal?

I ate some bizarre meals during my early attempts at abstinence. One of my three meals a day might be all potato chips and dip. I was struggling to forsake my old friend.

A healthy abstinence involves normal eating patterns. Some of us have never eaten normally and wonder, What is normal eating, anyway? Others of us barely recall normal eating patterns. It's like trying to recall an old song—we know bits and pieces of the words and melody, but we can't sing it. So here are some guidelines for normal, healthy eating that we can follow for the rest of our lives. You've seen many of these in print before.

Eat Only at Meal Time or Scheduled, Structured Snack Times Some people differ from a three-meals-a-day plan and plan only two meals a day. Still others allow for five small meals a day, which is especially good for hypoglycemic persons. Sandy kept her abstinence to three meals a day plus a cup of tea and a cracker before bedtime. At first this sounded weak to me, but I saw how radically difficult this was after we talked about how she used to eat double-decker sandwiches before she went to bed.

Eating a meal normally, I've learned, is . . .

- eating off a plate and sitting at a table, not eating out of containers in front of the refrigerator
- not snitching before, during, or after meal preparation
- enjoying fully the food you eat at meals
- eating slowly and pausing between bites
- not feeling stuffed after a meal
- eating a variety of foods, including ones that might have some fat or carbohydrates in them, such as breads and pasta.

Eat Moderate Meals Abstinence usually includes taking no second helpings, because much of our overeating consists of a pinch of this and a dab of that. "I'll have just a little bit more" turns into another meal. One helping (even if it's a little large at first) trains us not to return to food for more than sustenance. Stopping there even when we're hungry helps us gain time to let us feel how full we really are.

It's possible to eat only one helping and still overeat. Large first helpings bring back those old feelings of gluttony.

One thing that makes abstinence difficult to define is that in its purest form, it means abstaining from moments of gluttony. As we move along in abstinence and we become more aware of our drivenness, we can pinpoint these moments more easily. One example is the way many of us race through our meals because we're anxious to have that sensation of a full stomach.

Abstinence means slowing down and enjoying food as it was meant to be enjoyed. We don't, however, draw it out and make an event of it, either. Eating food at meals was never meant to fill our emotional tanks, just to sustain us physically.

Eat Balanced Meals A healthy abstinence includes meals that are balanced among grains and vegetables, fruits and protein. It limits sugar, refined carbohydrates, and high-fat foods, which are usually likely candidates as our binge foods. (If you need information about nutrition, read one of the many good books on that subject.)

As you dethrone binge foods, the healthier ones you've always hated take on a new appeal. I can even eat one of my most detested foods now, cottage cheese, without feeling as if I'm stuck in a concentration camp.

We can learn to set aside our appetite and sense how the foods we eat affect our energy level. It's an odd thought that food is simply a source of fuel for my body, not the main source of pleasure throughout the day.

In the beginning, it seems to be important not to skip meals. We're so afraid that we're going to be deprived that missing a meal scares us. Skipping meals can also create real hunger, which tempts us to gorge ourselves later to make up for the missed meal.

Eating that's normal involves a calm gratefulness instead of a needy drivenness about it. Consider the plight of the compulsive overeaters among the Israelites. They ate manna for forty years. They ate it fresh, baked, and boiled; each person was to gather only an "omer" (3.5 pints) of manna; if they gathered more, it became infested with maggots (Exod. 16:23; 16:35; 16:16, 20).

This is the stark reality of abstinence. Breakfast, lunch, and dinner are not controlled binges; they're simply occasions for sustenance. They enable us to live life as God intended, with love, laughter, purpose, and beauty.

Good-Bye, Dieting Behaviors

Those of us who are compulsive dieters have to be careful of diet-related feelings and behaviors. They tempt us to binge because we supposedly "deserve" the food.

Many of us need to make peace with the bathroom scales. We compulsive dieters have feared them or lived as slaves to them, letting them determine our self-esteem level and, therefore, our daily or hourly mood. If we did well, we felt good about ourselves. If not, we felt bad. Now scales are simply a tool to monitor our weight. Weighing once a month is enough. Some have had to throw their scales away and use the scales at their gym or doctor's office.

Focusing on weight loss can be harmful, too. In our dieting days, our progress or lack of progress in losing weight often acted as a flame to ignite our desire to eat:

- If I'd lost weight, I'd celebrate and have a cookie.
- If I hadn't lost weight, all hope was lost. I might as well give in and overeat.

If anything we do feels like a diet, we should either stop doing it or change our approach to it. For example, many diets suggest writing down everything we eat to discover problem areas.

That's not a bad technique, but we compulsive dieters use that kind of information to beat ourselves up. We must avoid any rigid, shameful dieting attitudes such as *I'm a bad person if I slip once.* They poison us with black-and-white thinking and distract us from the attitude of surrender. If a certain behavior isn't going to promote recovery, don't do it, no matter how wise it seems.

Respect Your Weaknesses

Watch Out for Trigger Moments We have times and places where we have eaten for years, and you might consider abstaining from eating during those times. Most compulsive overeaters are "night grazers," nibbling here and there from supper until bedtime. For me, the idea of not eating after dinner was a drastic one, but that has changed. Ten years ago, I "needed" something to eat before I went to bed to help me sleep; now if I eat something before I go to bed, I feel sick and can't sleep.

Another trigger moment is while watching television, since that's a prime snack time. At first, I had to hold a glass of iced tea just to watch television—now I can watch it empty-handed! I also try to avoid eating in the car because I tend to wolf down food there the way I used to when my car was a secret eating place.

Know Your "Point of No Return" If I buy potato chips, I'll eat too many of them. That means that if I pay for them at the supermarket, I've passed my point of no return. So I don't let it get that bad—I don't buy them.

If you can't walk past the freezer cases at the supermarket without buying ice cream, don't walk down that aisle. Get someone else to buy your frozen vegetables and juice. Don't assume you'll be strong—you're compulsive, remember? It isn't weak to avoid your "points of no return"; it's being rigorously honest about your weakness and helping yourself become abstinent.

The Broken Abstinence

I happened to call a recovering friend the day she broke a year of abstinence, and she told me about it.

"What are you going to do?" I asked.

"Go to a meeting tonight," she said. "All I ever had was one day—one day at a time. I'm turning over my compulsion and committing myself to one day at a time again."

I was glad for my friend's healthy model, because too often, breaking my abstinence became a reason to beat myself up. Gradually I learned that even though I didn't like sharing with my support group that I'd broken my abstinence, they would understand and accept me. I could start over.

There was still some healthy fear of breaking my abstinence, however. I didn't break it many times because I remembered how hard it was to start over, and I wanted to avoid that pain. Once I'd overeaten, I was tempted to put off starting my abstinence again. I don't use the phrase "losing my abstinence" because I don't believe that abstinent days are ever lost. Even if I break my consecutive string of days, those abstinent days are not lost to me. They showed me what it was like to think clearly and live a healthy life.

A broken abstinence isn't wasted, either. In those first ten tries over several months before I developed a continuing abstinence, I learned a lot about which foods triggered my overeating. When I overate, I sat down and thought about how uncomfortable my stomach felt and wished I hadn't eaten so much—this was a new feeling for me. I learned that I didn't have to be perfect to be loved by my support group, and I allowed myself to drink from God's love even when I goofed. I didn't give in to despair and thus fuel the addictive cycle.

When you break your abstinence, ask yourself questions:

- Have I discovered another binge food?
- Have I discovered another trigger moment?
- Have I discovered another point of no return?
- What was I feeling that made me want to eat?

Address the issue as soon as possible by journaling about it or calling your sponsor or a recovering friend. Hear the love and acceptance in their voices. Above all, pray and acknowledge that God still loves you in his accepting and relentless way.

Breaking our abstinence also reminds us that we are not the controllers. If we had only our own power, we could not be abstinent at all. Any abstinence, which is a miracle, is the work of God in us.

You May Be Wondering . . .

Q Is exercise part of abstinence?

A Exercising to enhance weight loss is a dieting behavior, so I won't exercise with the intensity or intention of weight loss. I believe that exercise helps your abstinence only when it has nothing to do with it.

Exercise may be part of recovery, however, because we learn to treat ourselves well when we exercise. To exercise is treat ourselves well because it helps us stay healthy and energetic. Exercise also helps us balance the mental and emotional work of recovery and can help us learn to be comfortable with our own bodies. It's a new thought to most compulsive eaters that exercise might even be fun, and that is a goal I'm now working on and even achieving at times.

Q Is it possible to work on recovery without working on abstinence?

A I don't think so, although many people try it. My experience is that working on recovery without working on abstinence denies us the clarity we need to feel our feelings and make wise decisions. We're trying to learn serenity, but it's blocked by our drivenness for food on the one hand and our sluggish hangover from overeating on the other. We may be in recovery, though, and not have several days of back-to-back abstinence. It often takes a while to become abstinent, and recovery begins when you commit yourself to using recovery tools. In the beginning, this may simply be coming to meetings.

SIX

Abstinent? Who, Me?

Imagine that you could have all your clothes specifically tailored to fit your body. Perhaps a clothes manager would keep a record of your body's idiosyncrasies, including the fact that your left foot is a half size bigger than your right. Finally, both of your shoes would fit your feet! Let's say you could get the pants for your suit two sizes bigger than the jacket without switching them in the store and feeling guilty. Wouldn't that be the best of all clothing worlds?

The Overeaters Anonymous guidelines for abstinence recommend that you tailor your abstinence to your compulsive eating idiosyncrasies. It's not a one-size-fits-all eating plan. The goal is to develop an abstinence that is workable for you, even if it's not ideal for the entire population.

WHO ARE YOU TO CHOOSE YOUR OWN ABSTINENCE?

How can compulsive overeaters be trusted to set their own abstinence? We're the "experts," so to speak, on our own compulsive eating tendencies. Even when we don't know them, we ask God to reveal our deepest compulsions with food, and we begin our surrender there. My basic compulsive eating behavior was that I snacked all day and into the night, so I asked God to help me find an abstinence to counteract that. It appeared one day in an OA brochure: *three meals a day and no second helpings.*

I thought that was too simple at first, but then I realized that simplicity is important because my compulsive eating and dieting had made my life complex. This simple abstinence tells us that we don't have to be pencil thin, we just need to maintain a healthy weight. It tells us we don't have to be either health food advocates or chocoholics, just normal, healthy eaters.

Choosing our own abstinence is good for our recovery because we are no longer passive receivers of treatment. The doctor or the nutrition counselor isn't handing us a diet and telling us to follow it. We are choosing for ourselves and trying to understand our body and our inner motivations.

Another reason that choosing our own abstinence helps us is that it reawakens and retrains our conscience. As a compulsive overeater, I had buried my conscience beneath my drive to eat. My decisions were clouded by time schedules (I've got to be home in time to eat), travel routes (I've got to shop today so I can pass my favorite convenience store), and social references (I'll ask Lindsay to go to lunch, because she'll munch out, too). Before recovery, my conscience was like a lawyer for the Mafia. It didn't speak up because I'd taught it to sympathize with my drivenness. It condoned, and even rationalized, my compulsive behaviors. Now that I've unearthed my conscience, I can trust it again. If a decision seems right, it may actually be right!

Some think this self-designing aspect of abstinence is fuzzy and unreliable, and it can be if you're not rigorously honest with yourself. I have found it empowering.

OPTIONS TO CONSIDER

Abstaining from Binge Foods

Even though Carla had been abstinent for several months, she still felt ruled by food. Every day she had to eat a chocolate bar from the candy machine at work as dessert for lunch. Every night she drank chocolate milk for dessert after dinner. Chocolate was enslaving her, so part of her abstinence was that she wouldn't have chocolate.

Many recovering compulsive overeaters abstain completely from trigger or binge foods, just as Carla abstained from all chocolate. Binge foods are usually salty foods such as chips, sweet foods such as cookies, or creamy foods such as chip dip.

Complete abstinence from a binge food may or may not be wise for you. According to Barbara McFarland, director of the Eating Disorders Recovery Center in Cincinnati, Ohio, "research indicates that the more a person restricts specific foods from her diet, the more likely she'll be to crave that food. Eventually, she'll give in to those cravings."[1]

Some of us eat chocolate and sugar when it is not excessive and it is part of a meal. For example, Sam designed his abstinence so that he may have candy bars, but not candy bars from the candy machine in his office building—they are too accessible and too tempting. Whenever we find a food that drives us, we add it to our abstinence until it loses its hold. Our goal is to eventually eat normally.

As I approached my first-year anniversary, I felt uneasy about my abstinence. I told this to Linnette, a Twelve-Step friend, who talked about how she abstained from foods to which she had been enslaved. As she spoke, the mental image of the rich and creamy chocolate cheesecakes that I made every Christmas appeared in my mind. I customarily made one for our family and others for friends. I had invested in several springform pans so I could make the cheesecakes just right. I'd almost broken my mixer trying to smooth the cocoa with nine packages of cream cheese. I received a lot of compliments for these cheesecakes. One friend even introduced me to people as the "one that makes those wicked cheesecakes." They were part of my identity!

As Linnette talked, I knew I could not make those cheesecakes that Christmas. I remembered that the previous year I had longed all day for my one token piece of cheesecake for dessert and how when I'd finished my piece, I'd lick my fork, my plate, and the knife I'd cut the cake with. I felt forlorn when every crumb was gone.

That Christmas I didn't make the cheesecakes, and I haven't made them again. I was sure I would miss them, but instead I felt playful freedom from food. With no cheesecake to ignite my cravings, I could focus on people and events, on spiritual issues of Christmas.

Refining Your Abstinence

The abstinence I began with is not as strict as my abstinence today. As my clarity and willingness have increased, I have abstained from more foods and activities because I now see that they are compulsive. Now that I eat so few sweets, I'm getting hooked on graham crackers (it's come to that!), so I limit the number I eat in one day. As I change and grow, so does my abstinence.

Knowing that you can add another behavior to your abstinence in the future means that you don't have to choose a perfect abstinence in the beginning. You have to start somewhere, so it's important to choose a workable abstinence and go for it. Start working your recovery—surrender, write an inventory, make amends, practice your conscious contact with God.

One helpful refinement of my abstinence has been to eat the same thing every morning for breakfast and the same thing for lunch unless I'm eating out. This sounds boring to many people, but for me, it has been one more effort at dethroning food. Since meals had become my only contact with food, I made a big event out of them. I cooked up scrumptious breakfasts, and I had dozens of pots and pans to wash, and after a while, I felt empty and frustrated because I was so preoccupied with food and unwilling to complete the addictive cycle. Now when I itch to fix an elaborate meal for breakfast or lunch, I tease myself, saying, "It's only breakfast, Jan. It's not the senior prom."

I've noticed that the times immediately after breakfast and lunch have become daily devotional and meditation times for me. I've never had time for these before, but my simple breakfast and simple lunch have created those time slots because I'm not fussing over food. I see now that when I sacrificed my preoccupation with food, I filled those moments with things that would advance my ever-growing desire to know and love God.

This simple food plan has also made it possible for me to maintain an abstinence without calling a food sponsor every day to report that day's menu. I am accountable to my Twelve-Step sponsor and to my support group on a regular basis, but I haven't had to make daily calls. My own style is that life seems more peaceful when I don't have to call someone every day. But when I find myself slipping, I make calls.

This illustrates how people respond to guidelines differently. Eating the same thing every day for breakfast and lunch might be too boring for you, and if so, don't do it. Calling a food sponsor every day may be necessary for you, and if so, do it. I believe we should show a lot of latitude and tolerance for others' ways of maintaining abstinence. A behavior that might wreck your abstinence could save someone else's.

But I Need More Structure

Some people feel they aren't ready for this kind of latitude, and they want a specific eating plan. They've been eating such huge portions for years that they have a distorted view of a normal-size portion. If you need such a specific eating plan, look for a sane one—no liquid diets, no thousand-calorie diets. Some people follow the Weight Watchers eating plan, while others participate in a variation of the OA program called OA-HOW. HOW stands for Honesty, Openness, Willingness. It puts more emphasis on structure in one's personal eating plan.

You can ask your doctor to supply a rational eating plan, especially if you have a specific dietary problem. Tell the doctor that this is not a diet but an eating plan for life.

Others May Not Understand

Abstinence is so foreign to our culture's approach to weight control that you can expect to be misunderstood by others (even doctors). It seems silly to people who don't understand compulsive overeating. When I'm asked if I'm on a diet, I say, "Not exactly," and then I change the subject. Explaining abstinence can be difficult, and I rarely do it because I'm no longer the chaos-creating crusader I was in my wildly compulsive days.

When I'm asked to eat something between meals, I rarely explain that the abstinence I've chosen doesn't include eating between meals.

I smile and say, "No, thank you," to

- "It's Friday. We always have doughnuts at work. Aren't you having one?"
- "Can't you have one lousy carrot stick?" (when it's not mealtime).
- "I made this cake just for you. Can't you have some?"

I don't defend myself, but I have wrapped up goodies and taken them home to my children to make people feel better. I don't give in, but I don't feel awkward, either. I can now listen to my conscience with peace that it's steering me down the right path. That's part of serenity.

Creating Your Own Abstinence

What will this mysterious abstinence look like, you wonder? Get all those perfectionistic, compulsive dieting tendencies out of the way by asking yourself: What would my ideal abstinence be?

Set that answer aside and finish the following sentences to help yourself define a realistic, helpful abstinence:

- Foods with which I get carried away are . . . (list in order of the severity of their attraction)
- Eating situations in which I get carried away are . . .
- Mealtimes become a problem when I . . .
- The last time I overdid it was . . .
- I feel most guilty about overeating when . . .
- I do/don't need a lot of structure because . . .
- Eating three moderate, balanced meals a day would/wouldn't work for me because . . .
- Having a scheduled, structured snack time would/wouldn't work for me because . . .
- Dieting behaviors that would be sure to foil my abstinence are . . .

- A basic abstinence (allowing for refinements later) would have to include at a minimum . . .

Try to pinpoint your most driven tendencies and consider whether they belong in your basic abstinence. Usually they do. For example, my primary compulsive eating behavior was continuous snacking, so three simple meals a day with no seconds was radical for me. That became my basic abstinence. As time has passed, I've added to my abstinence other behaviors and foods to avoid.

The most important feature of choosing your abstinence is to pray about it. It sounds like a cliché, but this is not a step to be overlooked. Bring all the above options before God and talk it over with him. You probably won't receive instant insight (although you might), but sit on these ideas for a few days. Give God a chance to provide you with a clear understanding of what would be the most beneficial abstinence for you.

STARTING YOUR ABSTINENCE

All this talk about abstinence and how to choose it brings us to the point where we need to think about "trying it on." What happens when I'm hungry? What should I watch out for? What if I break my abstinence? What are the surprises? Your first surprise may be that anger can help you.

A Touch of Anger

Anger, of all things, can boost us into abstinence. We're sitting in a heap with our brokenness all around us, and we've realized that our best friend—food—was actually our worst enemy. We feel betrayed, and so abstinence becomes our way of saying, "I'll show you!" or, "Wait until you see this!" to our former best friend. As long as we've surrendered, this healthy anger toward food breeds in us a quiet, useful determination.

I was so broken by my personal crises and my realization that food was strangling me that it took me a while to get this touch of determined anger. It began mounting as I tried about ten times to become abstinent only to break my abstinence within a few days or weeks. My anger blossomed out of a strange challenge.

One night while riding home from a meeting, my sponsor challenged me to try again. This nonconfrontive person was confronting me, and I felt irritated. Worse yet, it was mid-November, so if I began a lasting abstinence that night, I would miss the snacks and goodies of Christmas.

"I think you can do it," my sponsor said. By now I was angry, so I looked out the window to avoid eye contact.

Then it occurred to me that this could be an ironic turnaround. *Christmas,* I thought. *What a perfect time to slam the door on food—when my love affair with it is usually strongest.* I'd be getting revenge on my compulsive eating by getting my thirty-day "chip" during the Christmas season. The idea grew on me, and as we arrived at my house, I slammed the car door and ran in. I would give it another try. That was the night my lasting abstinence began.

I've seen that same healthy, quiet anger flash subtly or even well up boldly in the faces of my recovering brothers and sisters as they share in support groups. Then, the next week, I find out they're moving their way into abstinence.

No matter when you go for it, you're only working on today. Any time you leave a meeting is a good time to start your abstinence, since you've already got at least two hours of abstinence.

What Happens When I'm Hungry?

There are at least two types of hunger that occur between meals. One is not so much physical hunger as emotional and spiritual neediness for comfort and companionship. In these moments, we work through a stop-look-and-listen inventory, which will be described in the next few chapters.

Another type of hunger is our stomach's negative reaction to no longer being stuffed. We may check our inner issues and find that nothing is troubling us. We feel hungry out of habit. Some people address this hunger by drinking eight glasses of water a day, a practice that is recommended for good health. The three-meals-a-day abstinence discussed in OA usually allows drinking water, diet sodas, and other calorie-free drinks between meals.

Our fear of hunger lessens as we continue in recovery. After several years of abstinence, I had an interesting "peace talk" with my habitual hunger. I'd heard a lot about how we should "be with our hurt" when we were hurting, so I decided to try to "be with my hunger." I sat cross-legged on my living room floor, shut my eyes, and greeted the hunger as if it were a friend:

So this is what hunger feels like.

(I paused to feel the hunger.)

I'm not going to die from this hunger. I will get to eat dinner in an hour.

(I paused to shake hands emotionally with my hunger.)

I've repeated that scene a few times, and I find that being hungry isn't so threatening anymore. It's just there, and it will go away.

I share this not necessarily because I think you ought to do it, but I do think it's helpful to do things like it when they occur to you. As you trust yourself again, you may think of some seemingly odd ideas for refocusing your thoughts. Don't be afraid to try them.

WHAT TO EXPECT DURING ABSTINENCE

Most of us survive the early days of abstinence with a combination of strategies. We "white-knuckle" it sometimes. When we want to break our abstinence, we call recovering friends, we read the Twelve Steps, we quote Scripture. We do whatever it takes to get through the day, the next hour, the next thirty seconds.

I taped a copy of the Twelve Steps to a shelf next to the computer monitor where I worked every day and placed another copy in my purse. (They're both still in place.) Throughout the day, I'd read them and recite what I call "the surrender litany": "I can't, God can, so let him." An hour before lunch and dinner, I rehearsed this litany many times.

Some experience a "pink cloud abstinence" in their earliest days. Their surrender is so total that abstinence is easy, but it doesn't last for long because recovery is hard work. If this happens to you, take advantage of that total surrender by using recovery tools even if you don't feel that you need to do so. Then, when the pink cloud dissipates, you'll be more ready to work through the hard times.

New Insights

We ask ourselves why we're preoccupied with eating. Why are we sad? What are we afraid of? What personal neediness is crying out for attention that makes us yearn for the bandage our compulsion provides? These stop-look-and-listen inventories help us face our core issues instead of focusing so heavily on the behavior. They force us to reflect on why we're craving food.

Reawakened Feelings

We may have previously stuffed our anger, guilt, and fear, but now we must face them and express them as appropriately as we can. If we've never let ourselves feel angry before, we won't be tactful in our anger, and we may have to put on the brakes when we're tempted to chew out the telephone operator. It's better to talk angry moments over with a "safe" recovery friend. I made a lot of Twelve-Step calls in the beginning of my abstinence with questions like this: "I'm angry because my friend disciplined my kids. Is that appropriate? Should I tell her?" We rely on others with more recovery to help us express our feelings in healthy ways.

Mourning Food

For the first two years of my abstinence I dreamed regularly about all-you-can-eat salad bars and creamy cheesecakes. When I woke up from these dreams, I felt guilty, as if I'd broken my abstinence. I journaled about these dreams to relieve my unhealthy guilt.

We all have different ways of mourning food, just as we mourn when a friend moves away. St. Augustine described his struggles with casting off his old sins, especially lust: "The very toys of toys, and vanities of vanities, my ancient mistresses, still held me; they plucked at my fleshly garment, and whispered softly, 'Dost thou cast us off?' "[2] To which my answer is, "Just watch me!"

Visits from Angels

Especially in the earliest days of abstinence, I felt as if I had little guardian angels in charge of my abstinence. They seemed to pull little pranks to make it slightly easier. I would find that my favorite doughnut shop was closed in the middle of the day for no reason. Once the grill at my favorite hamburger stand was mysteriously not working. The convenience store had just run out of sour cream and onion potato chips, and I wouldn't settle for less. I would feel angry at first, and then I'd think about it. Finally, I'd chuckle and pray, "Another joke on me, right?" I was thankful that perhaps God had intervened in my behalf when I wasn't surrendering very well.

Midsentence Repentance

My old compulsive ways died hard, and I would find myself putting chips in my mouth and then spitting them out. At least once a week I pulled over to a fast food restaurant, parked, got out of the car, stood in line, and then turned around and walked out. On the way to the car, I would mutter, "I'm not promising that I'll never overeat again, but for this moment I won't."

This happened so often that after a while I quit even pulling over so much. When I did pull over, I stood in line and felt odd. I would silently ask God, "Are you going to make me leave this time?" However, I knew he wasn't forcing me to do anything, and I could imagine him saying, "Nobody's making you leave. Stay if you want." Then I'd chuckle and walk out.

I learned that it was never too late to decide not to eat, and many times my last-minute decisions saved my abstinence. If you've ever found a candy bar misplaced in the produce section of your grocery store, it's probably because someone like me put it there.

A New Freedom

Some compulsive overeaters experience a sense of peace in their first days of abstinence. Think of the bondage to which we're no longer enslaved. I no longer had to drive across town late at night for my favorite milk shake. I no longer felt tempted to take food off someone else's plate at a restaurant.

Abstinence was also freeing for me because I quit worrying about my weight. All I had to do was follow the eating plan of my abstinence and work on my recovery. The scales grew dusty.

If you're a typical compulsive overeater, abstinence scares you. You may find that beginning an abstinence feels as if you're walking off a cliff with no one to catch you. It is risk-taking faith walk. We wonder, *If I become abstinent, will God help me?*

God will be there, and it is there you will find that spiritual awakening as you let him do what you could not do for yourself.

You May Be Wondering . . .

Q How do I know if I'm being too hard on myself about my abstinence?

A Be careful of black-and-white thinking. When Maria took her chip for three years of abstinence, she said, "Actually, I probably have five years. I've been so hard on myself. For two years, I started over with every little slip, but I was basically abstinent. I wish now I hadn't done that because I beat myself up for nothing."

This isn't to say that we should have a sloppy abstinence. However, if for many months you gather several days and weeks but blow it and start over, perhaps you should set your sights a little lower and go for it.

SEVEN

What's Underneath It All?

Imagine this impossible mission: You've given a highly sophisticated psychological task to Person X, who has no training in psychology. Person X has a conflict of interest because he knows the patient involved and wants the patient to appear in the best light possible. Worst of all, Person X has to endure painful personal conflict to do this task, and his judgment is frequently clouded by compulsive desires.

This is the complex task you face when you write your own Twelve-Step inventory. You are the least qualified person to discover your self-destructive thought patterns, and you are also the most qualified. You have the most bias but also the most information about your own character.

In order to trust the outcome, you have to decide that in whatever way you write your inventory, you will be rigorously honest. You will dig out the character defects that have been in hiding for years. Your purpose is to move from self-delusion to self-honesty to self-acceptance.

WHAT IS AN INVENTORY?

A Twelve-Step inventory is a written account of your self-destructive thought patterns. It is a process of uncovering and naming character defects such as rage, selfishness, and dishonesty. Uncovering these defects helps us figure out what is driving us to eat compulsively.

It's called an inventory because we look behind the scenes to see what's filling the shelves of our mind and heart. We tally the damaged, out-of-date goods (unhealthy, habitual attitudes) and the desirable goods (healthy attitudes and strengths), which is why many people list their strengths in their inventory and this can help us remain objective.

Character defects are not the same as feelings, and an inventory doesn't ask you to deny your feelings or say they're bad. Character defects are patterns of self-destructive attitudes that feed negative, unhealthy feelings. Having a negative feeling is not the same as having a character defect. For example, sometimes I have feelings of regret that I wasn't in recovery when my children were preschoolers, but I've chosen not to live in that regret or let it color the way I look at life. I've abandoned the character defect of dwelling on the past. I forgive myself and do the best I can with my children now.

WHAT ARE WE LOOKING FOR?

When machines malfunction repeatedly, we know that a part isn't working properly. If we're wise, we repair the part instead of stringing a few rubber bands together to get the machine operating.

An inventory is an effort to figure out which parts need repair. Recovery involves taking those parts out and repairing and refinishing them. First, however, we look at how the machine is malfunctioning.

How have you been malfunctioning? What events and actions have taken place in your life that have gone wrong? These range from relationships we've abruptly ended to opportunities we passed by to times we've been obsessed with money. As you write about each event, consider your part in it. What character defect in you caused this or moved it along? Did you quit speaking to your sister because you were afraid to tell her how you felt? Did you neglect your duties on the job because you were angry with your coworker? Did the project fall apart because you repeatedly insisted on having your own way? Other persons involved may have displayed character defects as well, but that isn't your concern at this point.

These defects aren't the euphemized ones you usually hear casually shared in a prayer group. We identify the deep-rooted, ugly, unhealthy ways we respond to life and call them by their true names: not "exaggerating a little" but dishonesty, not impatience but intimidation, not "having a pity party" but self-pity. We use words that others don't like: resentment, pride, and manipulation.

In Twelve-Step groups, I saw new sides to self-centeredness. I had managed to take everything personally, as if things were always "done to" me. If my kids got a low grade on a report card, I didn't think about their feelings or their learning problems as much as I wondered how they could *do this to me.*

An important character defect that I didn't hear about until I attended Twelve-Step groups is grandiosity. This infrequently used word describes well the feigned grandeur and pretentiousness that so many of us display. It's that know-it-all attitude that makes you want to tape someone's mouth closed permanently because they seem to know all the answers. Grandiosity has many faces, as illustrated by these statements:

- I can see into other people's hearts and know their hurts.
- I know what's best for others and I will try to get them to do what I want.
- If they followed my advice, they could solve their problems.
- I can lick my overeating problem easily and without anyone else's help.

Support groups often shock newcomers because they hear behaviors confessed as they've never heard before, even in church: using people, fantasizing about the pastor, trying to be ultraspiritual just to get attention. That kind of honesty is bred by writing an inventory.

CAN I SKIP THE INVENTORY— PLEASE?

Many people put off writing an inventory because they don't like to write. An inventory isn't about writing; it's about you. No one will grade it for grammar or spelling; no one cares if the sentences are complete. You don't have to finish your inventory in one sitting—or even in ten. If you wish, you can do a little at a time. Just sit down and let it pour out.

Some people have said, "I've thought about what I should write, so I don't have to write it down." That sounds like something I, the great overanalyzer of all time, could have said. Thinking about it isn't enough, however.

The mysterious thing about writing our inventory or even journaling is that it isn't plain until it's written down. Our culture tells us to figure something out and then write it down. Inventories and journaling work the opposite way. You start in confusion, unaware of your defects, but your pen becomes your detective's hat. You uncover clues as you write, and when you're finished, you've solved some mysteries. As you write, you may have to go back and correct the parts that weren't as honest as they should have been.

Writing down our inventory provides a clarity we miss. To the confused and discouraged prophet Habakkuk, God said, "Write down the revelation and make it plain on tablets so that a herald may run with it" (Hab. 2:2). By writing it down, we make reality plain so that we're able to do something with it.

To skip the inventory is to hinder your recovery. For me, writing an inventory was one of the strongest breakthroughs. After that, there was no turning back. I knew the names of my enemies: self-pity, anger, and hostility, and I knew I would never be at peace with them again. Understanding these roots took away food's mysterious "healing" properties and set me on the journey I had needed to make for years.

WHAT METHODS ARE USED?

How we do our inventory makes little difference; what's important is that we do it. Twelve-Step programs are difficult and barely workable for those who are rigid and must do everything a certain way—the right way. An inventory drives them crazy because it can be done in many different ways. Like abstinence, the inventory is not a one-size-fits-all tool.

As a recovering controller, I needed this open-endedness. It forced me to set aside my clever methods and follow the direction of the Holy Spirit. Taking an inventory felt nothing like reading glib how-to books that told me how to become a whole person in six simple steps. In the Twelve-Step program, I've had to rely on God to fill in the gaps. Taking an inventory was one of those first leaps of faith that showed me that God could work even though I didn't have a foldout inventory chart with ten multiple-choice questions on it.

One frequently used method is to list troublesome events in your life and then look for the character defects you displayed during those events. When were your feelings hurt? When did you feel threatened? When did you resent others? In each case the goal is to write until you discover character defects. Then you write more about them—when, where, with whom, how, and why did they occur?

Here are some other methods that people have used:

- List your fears.
- List the times in your life when you were selfish, inconsiderate, or controlling.
- List (1) whom you feel resentful toward, (2) why you feel resentful, and (3) how that resentment now affects you.
- List the reasons why you overeat, such as anxiety, boredom, rage, loneliness, too many people around, too few people around, happiness, unhappiness, sex, lack of sex. For compulsive eaters, any reason is a good reason.
- List positive character traits—love, joy, peace, patience, kindness, goodness, faithfulness, gentleness, and self-control (Gal. 5:22–23)—and write about the situations in which you have violated them. Or list negative ones (Gal. 5:19–21) and the times you've acted them out.
- List the attitudes and actions that you dislike in others, leaving several lines under each. Do you dislike troublemakers, overreactors, status seekers, or people pleasers? Then write an incident about each in which you exhibited the same quality.

Many different kinds of inventories exist. For more examples, see the "Step Four" chapter of the book *The Twelve Steps of Overeaters Anonymous*. Choose a method that makes sense to you and use it. You can always write another inventory later, which is not unusual. If you keep listening to God, he may reveal to you several times that you need to write another inventory.

Some people worry so much about doing their inventory "right" that they never do it at all. This completely misses the point. If you have a sponsor, ask him or her for suggestions. Recovery is a team effort. There are only a few tools you will use alone.

Positive Inventories

Many people also list their positive qualities in the inventory, and this can be helpful, particularly if you beat yourself up a lot. You could list the fruit of the Spirit and ask yourself, When have I shown these qualities? Then, through this positive lens of self-examination, you can ask, When do I need to show them more?

You can list the strengths you see in yourself based on your successes. Be careful to identify your true strengths, not just the things you've done to please others. Many of us have catered to others' wishes for so long that we don't know our true strengths and gifts.

The counsel I was given when I wrote my initial inventory was to write the story of my life, highlighting the troublesome events in it. I was advised to notice how I responded to each event as I wrote about it and to write the character defect it showed in the margin. I was even told that it would get boring after a while because the same character defects would pop up in the margin over and over. This happened.

I started with my earliest memories and tried to tell about troubling situations in which I was afraid or angry. For example, at the age of three I hid under my mother's office chair during storms in fear of thunder and lightning. As I wrote about it in my spiral notebook, I could sense that I was living my life under my mother's chair: afraid to take chances; afraid the worst would happen; afraid that God, the creator of thunder and lightning, wasn't a good guy after all. These are character defects, not because I felt them as a three-year-old but because I let them dominate my adult life.

I followed the tone I'd heard in my support group, and I didn't concern myself with the offenses of others. I tried simply to see what happened, how I reacted, how I felt. I wrote sentence fragments about birthdays, childhood friends, and teachers. I wrote my feelings about my parents, about having to move, about how I looked and dressed. After a while, I stopped and found I was exhausted, so I read over my inventory and began making those notes in the margins.

I watched the prediction come true: I was bored. Out in the margin these same words reoccurred: self-pity, anger, laziness, self-doubt. Intermittently, I had made notes that said:

- misrepresented facts
- made others feel guilty
- said things I didn't mean in anger
- relied on outward looks alone

I was stunned at the patterns I'd discovered. I hadn't thought of myself that way before. I could see why my compulsive overeating had been so necessary in my life—I had a lot to ignore.

TOPICAL INVENTORIES

After you've completed your character inventory, you may want to do a compulsive eating inventory. Most of us take a historical approach by outlining the start and progression of our compulsive eating. The purpose of this inventory is to "clean out your closet" and air your sick secrets about food. You may want to answer questions such as:

- What were the circumstances that surrounded the onset of your compulsive eating?
- How old were you when this happened?
- How did you come up with the idea to overeat?
- How did it progress?
- What have been your dieting experiences?
- How do you feel answering these questions?

Another version of a compulsive eating inventory can include all the reasons you don't want to be slim. Is that ridiculous? Many compulsive eaters harbor reasons for wanting to be overweight—not wanting to be bothered sexually, not wanting people to expect a lot, not bothering with how we look because it seems too hopeless to try. Some of us who are single fear rejection so much that we don't date; if we're married, we don't attempt to build an intimate relationship with a spouse because we don't want to risk the vulnerability required. Some compulsive eaters don't know how to feel anything but worthlessness, and they would feel naked without that extra weight.

Compulsive eaters often need to write an inventory about sexuality. In this inventory, we detail negative behaviors and character defects. Sexuality and food are often intertwined in a subtle, quiet way as eating becomes a "safe" replacement when sex is too scary for us. If you've run from a healthy sex life with your spouse, you may want to write this inventory. It's also a good idea for those who have struggled to stick with the standards for sexual behavior they have chosen. Violating sexual boundaries over and over again creates a shame that is difficult to shed.

MY SIDE OF THE STREET ONLY

But what if some of the events we write about aren't our fault? What do we write?

We sort out what was our fault, and we own that part. The philosophy of Twelve-Step recovery is expressed in the analogy of "cleaning up my side of the street and letting others clean up theirs." With situations in which people lied to me or even cheated me, I write about how I responded. Did I gossip about them, possibly to get revenge? Did I try to intimidate them? Did I take advantage of them in some way?

This isn't a self-blaming attitude but a problem-solving one. We can't do anything about another's problem, but we can take responsibility for our own behavior. We don't have to shift the responsibility to others who harmed us. We quit simply reacting to others, and we make choices about our attitudes.

This my-side-of-the-street attitude carries over into all of life, which my sponsor modeled well for me. When someone we knew may have been displaying a character defect, my sponsor would say, "I'm not going to take their inventory. I don't know the whole story, so I'm not going to judge." For a critical person like me, this was the model I needed. It is never my job to take another person's inventory. And who would want to? Taking my own was and is painful enough.

Leftovers from Childhood

Some of us find that instead of writing our own inventories, we write our family's inventory instead: "I overeat because my mother forced me to clean my plate." This may be true, especially because eating disorders are generally family diseases, but at this point we focus on our own character defects. There is a time and a place for recovery from wounds of our dysfunctional family, but at this moment we're taking responsibility for our character defects.

We may have also developed some of our defects as mechanisms to protect ourselves, but now we've made them life patterns. For example, Stacey frequently lied to stay out of trouble with her harsh, overbearing father. Lying became her coping mechanism to avoid unreasonable punishment, but now, in adulthood, Stacey lies when it would be just as easy to tell the truth.

In Stacey's inventory, she focused on how she had gone overboard to protect herself:

- I stuff myself to get rid of hurt.
- I push others away because I'm afraid of intimacy.

Too often, we have turned the pain of our past into harm toward others. We keep using our former protective mechanisms, and they turn on us just as food has.

In our inventories, we take responsibility for these continuing overreactions to the hurts we've encountered. We can't control the behavior of the person who hurt us, but we can control our response as we surrender our character defects to God.

Q How do I take my inventory without beating myself up?

A We're not attorneys looking for convictions, just detectives searching the hideouts in our personalities. Quiet the perfectionistic "king baby" part of you that wants to condemn you, or it will destroy your search for clues. Pursue rigorous honesty but not shame. As you write about situations, you may want to tell what you did well in addition to how you failed so you present a balanced view of yourself.

You may feel some healthy guilt, though. Even after writing an inventory that is honest but not self-blaming, you don't feel in a party mood. Over the years we've listened to sermons about these defects, and an inventory is something like the defendant standing before the judge and entering the plea "guilty." In whatever way God leads you to take your inventory, he will provide the sufficient grace for you to accept all that you discover about yourself.

Recovery involves accepting reality but not being defeated by it. We're after progress, not perfection. The recovery phrase "easy does it" refers to the way that we allow God's grace to be imparted to ourselves on a daily basis. We see God's problem-solving, easy-does-it, one-day-at-a-time approach in Isaiah 43:18–21. When the Israelites had been faithless, God told them to repent. What was his next command?

- He reviewed the best point in their relationship (vv. 16–17).
- He told them to forget their former faithlessness (v. 18).
- He challenged them to see that he was working and nurturing them (vv. 19–21).

This is how we also react after we've completed our searching and fearless moral inventory: challenged by our future but not destroyed by our past.

EIGHT

Making the Most of My Inventory

Before writing our inventory, we saw a distorted image of ourselves through a smudged and speckled mirror. Our inventory cleaned that mirror, wiping away the smudges and specks. As we gaze at our true image in this clean mirror, we see our problems for what they are, and we can even name them.

We think of ourselves differently after writing our inventory. We can't erase the images it has planted in our minds. It's as if our inventory becomes a living thing that stays with us. In reality, our reawakened conscience has gotten a glimpse of our true image, and it wants to repair that image.

To keep this image from haunting and defeating us, we continue to walk through recovery and surround ourselves with others who are doing the same. We make our inventory count by cleaning the mirror as soon as it gets smudged with rationalizations and excuses.

WHAT DO I DO WITH THIS INVENTORY?

First, we present the results of our inventory to God (Step Five). As I finished writing my inventory, I reviewed my character defects and recited them to God. This was humbling because I'd been mad at him for a long time, and now I was not only surrendered but also willing to admit how I had been wrong. I felt like the prodigal daughter come home. I remember closing my prayer with a sad smile and saying, "I guess none of this is new to you, is it? Thank you for loving me no matter what."

To Ourselves

Admitting my character defects to myself took several weeks. Whenever I moved into the preoccupation phase of the addictive cycle, I recalled the character defects I'd penciled in the margins of my spiral notebook. *This isn't about cheese and crackers,* I'd think. *This is about self-pity.* I admitted my defects to myself over and over.

To Another Human Being

Perhaps it's a little easier to admit your character defects to someone else after you've admitted them to God and to yourself. When I read my inventory aloud to my sponsor, I felt humiliated at first, but I found that was unnecessary. Human frailty is so common that I felt right presenting myself as I really am. My sponsor accepted me in spite of my faults. Soon, I easily listed the defects for my support group, and I was surprised to see so many eyes widen and heads nod in agreement.

Because reading our inventory involves so much risk, we may choose to read it to whomever we like. I felt honored when a single recovery friend chose to read her sex inventory to me. In it she chronicled the times she had stood by her convictions and the times she'd zoomed past them. She had struggled so much to follow God, yet she was so honest about her failures. She buried her head in her paper as she read, so she was surprised to look up and find that I was crying, too. When she read about leading men on, I began to wonder if I had done this in ways so subtle I hadn't recognized it before. We ended up crying and holding each other for a long time. She prayed and asked for God's forgiveness, and it was exciting to see her accept his forgiveness and then to forgive herself, too. This became a turning point in her recovery.

Admitting character defects becomes a way of life. We become people who freely admit our faults instead of hiding them, which helps us dismiss those illusions of perfectionism.

ECHOES OF MY INVENTORY

Writing my inventory and reading it to someone else meant that I was ruined, so to speak, to my compulsive eating and the game was over. I could no longer indulge in a self-pity jag or an angry outburst because I saw how these defects had hurt my relationships and cost me career advancements. I could no longer let others suffer for my grouchiness.

I eagerly asked God to remove these defects of character (Step Six), using my surrender litany (Steps One through Three) over and over on my defects. I admitted my powerlessness over my anger or my self-pity and turned them over to God, who was everything but powerless.

I knew I was willing to let go of my character defects (Step Seven) when I began plotting against them. When I felt angry, I developed a strategy for how I could talk about a problem without blaming or yelling at anyone. In my journaling, I wrote about how I could handle the same problem better the next time. I figured out how I could have expressed my own needs better or how I could have set aside my own hurts for the moment and cared for someone else. That rehearsal in writing equipped me to handle difficult situations better the next time. Perhaps not right, but better.

Still, it's tough to be willing to let go of character defects. We find ourselves playing tug-of-war with God because we're not ready to say good-bye. Sometimes we even feel trapped—how can we stop these old behaviors? My lying protected me; my status seeking gave me self-worth (albeit false); my rage helped me get my point across! Romans 7:23 says that we are prisoners of the law of sin at work in us. Sin dwells in us, and we've made it feel at home there. We have a hard time letting it go, so we jump in and out of surrender all day, finally relinquishing each defect. The more we let go, the less imprisoned and driven we feel. A quietness takes over, and even though we're dying to eat, we find we can let go of that, too.

MAKING A LIST

After writing my inventory, I knew I had to make the list of people I had harmed (Step Eight) and then make amends to them (Step Nine). Making amends means that we restore what we have taken. Sometimes this means financial restitution; other times, it's clearly admitting we're wrong and stating how we intend to change.

I went to my husband and then to my six- and seven-year-old children individually and asked their forgiveness. I explained that I intended to stop criticizing them and that I would treat them with the kindness they deserved. My husband said little; I knew he was waiting to see some changes.

That one-time admission was nothing compared with the daily admissions that occurred as I caught myself getting angry, being lazy, and making family members feel guilty. It became routine for me to say:

- That was an unkind thing for me to say. I'm sorry.
- I was wrong to be so impatient with you. Can we start over?
- I blamed you when it wasn't your fault. That was wrong.

It became something of a game to catch myself more quickly so I didn't have to bore my family with yet another apology. All three of them eventually saw changes in me, changes that I'm sure will keep happening for the rest of my life.

Checking It Twice

I tried to brush aside making a list of those I'd harmed outside my family because I had done something similar to that several years before. At that time, I'd apologized to several friends, to an old boyfriend, and to one of my parents, so I figured I was off the hook.

However, I watched my recovering friends. One was paying back thousands of dollars he owed, and another was donating money to a charity because she couldn't locate the person she had harmed. Their actions inspired me, so I made a list, but there weren't too many people on it, and the ones I did list didn't count because everything was their fault anyway.

As time passed, I saw that everyone on the list did count and that some things were my fault. I asked God's forgiveness for my actions. Then I went to each person, and each generously received me. I held back with one person. He was a relative who rarely spoke to me although he had once liked me. At first, I told myself it didn't matter, but I was learning to ask myself, What is the truth? What is my responsibility? I could think of a time he had gotten angry with me. Which of my character defects had shown itself?

I threw that question up to God, and within a few weeks I couldn't get away from the realization that once again my grandiosity had caused me problems. I remembered that this person had gotten angry with me when I had been trying to convince him of something that was foreign to him. I thought I was right, so I kept pushing. It seemed that after that everything I did irritated him. My defect was my know-it-all grandiose attitude.

I planned what I would say to him. Yuck. This was a person who talked a lot, but never about feelings. He didn't even look people in the eye when he spoke to them. How would he respond to my admission of guilt and request for forgiveness? Was this too touchy-feely for him? Would he yell at me again? Or would he say that he didn't know what I was talking about? I was scared. So I began. "I'm calling to say that I have been wrong, that I have been pushy and insisted on having my own way. Would you forgive me?"

Silence.

Then, "Sure thing."

Then he said that he hoped our financial situation would work out soon (my husband had left the ministry and was laid off from his subsequent job) and that our lives would take a better direction.

Since then, I have treated this person kindly and gone out of my way for him several times. If he and I see things differently, I don't comment on it. I now feel content to listen because I'm not so worried about expressing my opinion or getting my point across.

Still, there are times when I get frustrated with the way he treats people. Since my apology, he has told others that I am a mean, hateful person, but I've surrendered that to God. Doing that was difficult, but not as difficult as before. He apparently doesn't choose to acknowledge that I've changed. I wish it weren't that way, but it doesn't eat me up because I'm not a people pleaser anymore. I still have many faults, but what he said isn't true, and I know that. I'm free to see him objectively as a person with good and bad qualities who chooses to dislike me.

MY-SIDE-OF-THE-STREET AMENDS

We can't worry about whether the people to whom we make amends will forgive us. We aren't making amends to please them or even to restore our relationship with them, although those things might happen. Our goal is to clean up our side of the street. We can't worry about the other side of the street (the other person's defects) or even about how the street looks (the relationship). We cleanse our conscience, make restitution if necessary, and change our behavior toward that person.

Our apology has to be more than saying "I'm sorry." To be clear, we need to acknowledge that we were wrong by saying "I was wrong to . . . ."

We avoid excuses or elaborate explanations, and we offer our sincere regret. If we've left the mistaken impression that we didn't care about that person, we correct that and reassure them about how important they are in our lives.

What if making amends will do more harm than good? I've watched recovering friends struggle with whether they should tell their spouse of previous emotional and even sexual attachments. If they told their spouse, would the spouse be able to live with this? Would the spouse say that he or she could but then dwell on it afterward?

Sometimes we tell ourselves that our apology would do more harm than good because we simply don't want to make amends. Once again, recovery is teamwork. We talk this over with our sponsor or therapist or pastor or recovering friends to gain some objectivity. We ask, Do I sound as if I'm afraid to make amends? Do you think this person would be harmed by my apology? You might even rehearse your apology with a recovering friend, pretending he or she is the person you have harmed, and then ask, How did you feel hearing this apology? Were you harmed in any way?

Backing into Serenity

Making amends can be humiliating, but that can be powerful. I have made amends so many times now that I avoid it by not getting myself into situations in which I will have to make amends to someone. I've withheld sarcastic remarks and delayed making emotionally charged telephone calls so I won't have to make amends for smart remarks. I set aside judgmental feelings before they develop into a negative attitude. I wish I could say I've done this because I'm becoming a kinder, more serene person, but that's not entirely true. I'm surrendering my need to criticize, and that's about all.

Am I putting up a false front? I think not. Serenity and kindness have not come naturally, so I "fake it till I make it," as they say in AA. That means not that I pretend to be something I'm not but that I learn by doing. The more I practice having serenity, the more I seem to acquire it. I agree to surrender my smart comments and see what happens; I'm usually happy with the results. I have a feeling that serenity and kindness are going to sneak up on me when I'm not looking.

DAILY INVENTORY TAKING

Another valuable pattern is to review our behavior and attitudes and pinpoint character defects and character strengths we showed that day. We ask, Was I selfish, resentful, or fearful? We surrender those defects and, if necessary, make amends as soon as possible (Step Ten). We pray for those toward whom we feel greed or suspicion or impatience, asking for God to bring into their lives the same good things we want for ourselves. This process cleans up our side of the street, and, to my amazement, it releases negative feelings toward others.

Recognizing our progress is important, too. Which strengths, through God's grace, have we shown today? Thanking God for this progress spurs us on in our recovery. Here's a list of both kinds of qualities you might want to use in your daily inventory.

Character Defects	*Character Strengths*
fearful	courageous
rash	discerning
greedy	compassionate
lazy	creative, resourceful
inconsistent	dependable
rigid	flexible
resentment	forgiveness
biased	fair
stingy	generous
harsh, callous	gentle, sensitive
proud	humble
ungrateful	thankful
self-pity	self-forgetfulness
self-justification	humility
self-importance	modesty
suspicion	trust
doubt	faith
disrespectful	courteous
anger	serenity
deceitful, exaggerating	truthful
selfish, self-seeking	attentive to others
lustful	concerned for others
impatient	patient
gluttony	moderation

We don't allow the time when we take these daily inventories to become times to beat ourselves up. We take them with the heart knowledge that we are loved by God and that he shows those bountiful qualities toward us, even when we are less than we could be.

RENEWING THE MIND: STOP-LOOK-AND-LISTEN INVENTORIES

One way we surrender these defects is to take a stop-look-and-listen inventory when we feel hungry (Step Ten). Instead of eating, we ask ourselves what we're feeling or reacting to and what character defect is in operation. The results of our fourth step inventory usually come back to us, and we know what's going on inside us—fear, guilt, anger. Instead of numbing out, we confess these feelings and ask God to remove them, using whatever tools are necessary.

Shortly after I wrote my fourth step inventory, I wrote in my journal about a situation in which I battled my feelings. I was feeling grouchy and sorry for myself because nothing was going as I'd planned. I was riding in the car with my family, and there was no food within reach to make me feel better.

Since I refused to take my self-pity and grouchiness out on my children or husband, I felt as if my head would explode. I stared out the window and cried, but doing so quietly so I wasn't enlisting pity from my husband. As I stared, I turned over my grouchiness, my desires, my supposed right to have a perfect day, to God and asked him to help. Finally I leaned my head back on the headrest, shut my eyes, and "rested" in God. This was one of the first times I ever faced my grouchiness and worked through it instead of venting it on others. It set an important pattern in my life.

Don't be discouraged if these stop-look-and-listen inventories reveal the same defects over and over. This is where we fight the battle of preoccupation with food, and these quick thinking inventories short-circuit the addictive cycle. Expect these battles to occur frequently as you undo a powerful addictive pattern in your life.

Humility is the key to patience with ourselves, and this forced humility fosters more recovery. We become more aware of our brokenness, and we're less likely to think we can solve our problems by eating. And it's exciting. God is doing for us what we cannot do for ourselves.

The next few chapters examine the major parts of this stop-look-and-listen inventory. Declaring war on the enemy means asking ourselves:

- How do I *feel* (Chapter 9)?
- What do I *think?* Is a myth or character defect behind this feeling? What is the truth in this situation (Chapters 10, 11)?
- What will I *do?* What tools am I going to use to recover the truth? (Chapters 12, 13)? What am I going to do to avoid sabotaging my recovery (Chapters 14–18)?

You May Be Wondering . . .

Q Is it ever appropriate to make amends to myself?

A Yes. Often the people we have harmed most are ourselves. Our names could be at the top of our lists. We have beat ourselves up; we have isolated ourselves; we have riddled ourselves with shame. At this point, we may need to make amends to ourselves by making decisions about how we will talk to ourselves: Will I heap guilt on myself? Will I call myself names? We choose to take care of ourselves by allowing time to do the things we love, by acknowledging our achievements. If you're part of a support group, take those tokens of recognition and let others' compliments sink in.

NINE

Making Friends with Feelings

In one of the first OA meetings I attended, someone said that compulsive overeaters haven't grown emotionally beyond the age at which they began eating compulsively. According to this, if you began overeating when you were eight, you have progressed little beyond the emotional maturity of an eight-year-old.

Our emotional growth is handicapped from that time because that's when we started using food to boost our spirits on a regular basis. We stopped coping with our feelings and looking for ways to solve problems. At the age of fourteen, I began finding dirty saucers and empty pretzel bags under my bed from my late-night runs to the kitchen. At thirty-two, I often behaved with the emotional maturity of a fourteen-year-old.

Perhaps this is why in recovery I relived my adolescence, learning to interact socially and becoming more interested in grooming and dress. I also experienced the mood swings of an adolescent as I faced the full range of my emotions for the first time in my life.

EMOTIONS: THE STRANGERS WITHIN

It seems uncomfortable to have to make friends quickly with a stranger, especially one who talks a lot. We feel that same awkwardness toward our emotions in recovery. We don't speak their language.

They may be too loud or too expressive. We're not sure we want to get acquainted with them.

The first step in the stop-look-and-listen inventories we use when we want to eat compulsively is to ask ourselves, *What am I feeling? What am I trying to prove to myself? Is this feeling related to my known character defects or to a new one I'm about to discover?*

Getting acquainted with our emotions is a layered process much like making friends with strangers. First we meet them, then we remember their names, then we like being around them, and finally we get to know them. In the same way, we acknowledge feelings, identify them, accept them, and finally express them.

ACKNOWLEDGING FEELINGS: "IT'S NICE TO MEET YOU"

In the past, we buried our emotions, wished them away, and refused to feel them because we didn't want to be blamers, whiners, or screamers. As we attempt an abstinence, however, buried emotions come up, and they force us to acknowledge them or to stuff ourselves.

Some of us routinely ignore feelings because we were taught to stop crying and cheer up. "That's why it's a new thought to compulsives to allow discomfort," says psychiatrist Edward Khantzian, Ph.D., a professor at Harvard Medical School.

> We need to get rid of the fear of discomfort and accept that distress is an inescapable part of life. Dysfunctional families [and most families are dysfunctional to some degree] either ignore the children's negative feelings or tell children to keep these feelings to themselves. This can be changed by staying with the hurt and knowing that there isn't relief to every hurt.[1]

But we're afraid of the way these emotions interfere with our work and relationships. *If I get real emotional, I'll turn that person off,* we think. We're afraid we won't fit in if we acknowledge our feelings, so we ignore them.

But emotions don't stay buried. They leak, so to speak, and we find ourselves saying and doing things we regret. When my husband was laid off, I felt angry because his boss had promised him his job would be spared. I thought I'd taken care of this anger until I found myself sniping at a dawdling customer in line at a department store.

As soon as I spoke, I looked around to see who had made that irritated comment. Was it me? Within a few minutes, I realized that I had projected my anger over the layoff onto this unsuspecting customer. Psychiatrist Gerald May explains: "Something that has been repressed does not really go away; it remains within us, skirting the edges of our consciousness. Every now and then it reminds us of its presence, as if to say, 'Remember me?'"[2]

Our goal is to sit quietly and say to ourselves, Yes, I feel strange, and I'm going to see what it's all about. Just as you sit with a grieving friend, sit quietly and be with your feelings. If we hurt, we need to let ourselves hurt. That way our emotions are no longer a bogeyman over us. The pain heals and dissipates. It's one application of, "You will know the truth, and the truth will set you free" (John 8:32).

You might say it's too painful to acknowledge your feelings. Consider that it may be more painful to block the feelings and yell at unsuspecting people in department stores. Or, even worse, you can let negative emotions skirt your consciousness so you feel compelled to overeat.

IDENTIFYING FEELINGS: "I KNOW YOUR NAMES NOW"

Since we don't usually acknowledge our feelings, we're not skilled at identifying them, either. Usually, the feeling is related to a character defect, so we can often identify the emotion more easily if we've written an inventory.

What if we feel many emotions at once—confusion, fear, irritation? There are several paths through this. One is asking this simple question: Am I mad, sad, or glad? We mull over recent events in our life until the feeling gets stronger, and that may be the trigger event. (Sometimes, however, that confusing feeling is simply tiredness, and we need to rest.)

Another path is to name what part of your body hurts. Does your neck ache? Is your stomach tight? Once you can explain how your body hurts, you can sometimes explain your feelings, too.

Many times I unravel my emotions by journaling. I keep at it until I've uncovered all of them and I feel better. I don't want to be left with a residue of unidentified negative feelings.

When nothing else seems to work, a release of physical energy usually does. I take a break from "living in my head" to jump on my bike for a ride in the wind or wrestle with my kids. When I am done, things usually make more sense, and when they don't, I put the process on hold. Usually by the next day I can easily name my feelings.

Naming our emotions is important because it gets them out there where we can see them. It dissolves some of our panic because we're no longer so baffled.

Anger wears so many disguises that it can be difficult to identify. You may express your anger by crying or getting quiet or running away or getting loud and violent. Grief often disguises itself as anger. Sometimes I become frustrated about something and suddenly realize how much I need to cry. I'm not angry as much as I'm grieving over a loss of someone or something.

ACCEPTING FEELINGS: "I LIKE BEING AROUND YOU"

Some of us who are enslaved to being looking-good kids panic at the thought of being frustrated and upset, so on top of being angry or afraid, we're panicked that we're angry or afraid!

Fighting stress makes it worse. "We get anxious about being anxious," says Edward Khantzian, who is also the principal psychiatrist for substance abuse disorders at the Cambridge Hospital. "Distress is not the enemy; it's trying not to have it that thwarts us."[3]

Accepting a feeling can be difficult when we don't understand its source. At this point, we need to acknowledge the complexity of our emotions and accept them anyway. Too often, I've spun my wheels because I'm upset and can't figure out why.

Then I get more frustrated. This is a form of fighting the feeling rather than going with it. Sometimes it's OK to say that feelings just are. This is one more way to surrender and to admit that we don't know everything.

EXPRESSING FEELINGS APPROPRIATELY: "LET'S GET TO KNOW EACH OTHER"

Expressing emotions is scary to many of us. How can we be with our hurt without becoming so depressed we can't stand it? How can we tell people how we feel without sounding harsh or self-pitying? How do we express anger appropriately without wounding others?

Appropriateness involves safety. We find safe activities, groups, and people with whom we can express hurts even if they seem unfair or ugly. As we watch others, we learn to express negative emotions in constructive ways, which is a key to reworking our character defects. We don't blame, but we own our emotions by saying "I feel this way" instead of "You make me feel this way." We gain some understanding of what it means to be angry but do not sin by holding grudges or taking our anger out on others (Eph. 4:26).

"Safe" activities and people are ones in which we feel loved and accepted as compulsive eaters, ones in which no one is shocked by our behavior and no one shames us. Here are some safe activities and people with whom you can express your emotions.

Crying

Some of us have refused to cry for many years and have ignored this powerful, God-given release. We fight it because we don't want to embarrass ourselves or take the time to have a good cry. "By crying, we're not kidding ourselves about our distress," says Dr. Khantzian. "We're dignifying hurt with our own attention."[4]

During my first thirty days of abstinence, I felt so many strange emotions that I cried every day. I became worried that my crying was harming my children, so I retreated to my bedroom to cry and journal. If they came in, I explained that we all need to cry sometimes and this was one of those times for me. My crying didn't mean that they had done anything wrong.

Gut-Level Honest Prayer

Prayer can be a place in which we reveal our darkest secrets and deepest feelings to God. We tell God whom we're mad at and why (even if it's God!). We list for him the impossibilities of doing our job, of staying married, of working our recovery.

There are times when talking to others will not help—only talking to God will. Think about Hannah of the Old Testament, who was childless while her husband's other wife, Peninnah, had many sons and daughters. With Peninnah making fun of Hannah and her husband mouthing trite cliches, Hannah took her grief to the temple in prayer. Imagine Hannah praying with words so slurred and gestures so exaggerated that the priest Eli mistook her fervency for a drunken stupor. Hannah simply explained: "I was *pouring out my soul to the Lord*" (1 Sam. 1:15b).

This prayer equipped Hannah to respond instead of react to Peninnah's gibes, her husband's botched comfort, and Eli's mistaken impression. This type of praying accommodates the fountains of our emotions and allows us to surrender them to God for his control rather than letting them control us.

Some of us are afraid to tell God how we honestly feel. Our imperfect feelings embarrass us, so we try to hide them—as if God won't know about them unless we tell him! Others are afraid they're being irreverent if they grumble to God about how exasperated they are with their boss or their children or bureaucratic red tape. Yet David presented all kinds of emotions to God, even the ones that weren't pretty:

Depression: "I am worn out from groaning; all night long I flood my bed with weeping and drench my couch with tears" (Ps. 6:6).

Doubt: "How long, O Lord? Will you forget me forever? How long will you hide your face from me?" (Ps. 13:1).

Revenge: "Let death take my enemies by surprise; let them go down alive to the grave, for evil finds lodging among them" (Ps. 55:15).

These sentiments do not reflect the pearly-white smile of the looking-good Christian whose facade is in place. They were written by a simple "man after God's own heart" laying himself bare before God (Acts 13:22).

Because God listened to David's ranting and raving, we know that he will not be ruffled by our ridiculous feelings. This makes him the ultimate one to whom we can confess. He listens to the full intensity of our rage. He doesn't overlook our meanness, but he looks deep into it and forces us to do the same. Together we explore the worst parts of ourselves and find the acceptance we crave in his acceptance of us. God helps us discover the answers ourselves, as evidenced by the way David's saddest Psalms often ended in confident praise of God.

This coming around to a place of praise keeps us from being irreverent. Irreverence is railing without apologizing, complaining without thanking, stretching the facts without correcting them. As we unloose our emotions, we are responsible for staying honest and fair. As we gripe and fume, we tone down our exaggerations. We can't fool God because he sees things as they are.

These episodes leave us with a closeness to him much like we have after pouring out our hearts to friends. When we seem weak, we look back to our conversations with him and draw on them for strength.

Support Groups

Negative emotions, even if they seem wrong or untrue, can flow freely in a support group because no one fixes us with advice or slaps a Scripture verse on us. Our support group friends don't look away or interrupt us; instead, they lean forward to listen. Many times I hang my head as I share what I think is the most disgusting feeling only to look up and see half smiles and nodding heads. These people feel the same emotions I feel and do the same things I do. This freedom of expression helps us hear ourselves more objectively and sort out what is fact and what is falsehood.

In support groups, we hear others describe their feelings, and what they say "clicks"—that's what we've been trying to say! They've named our feeling for us. I spotted my know-it-all attitude first by hearing other group members talk about theirs, and then I realized I acted the same way. Other times I've watched people meander through topics until they hit upon what's bothering them, and then they speak it out and release it.

All these things are possible because support groups require confidentiality (you may not reveal who attended or what is said), which produces the possibility for rigorous honesty. At first, we may have difficulty expressing our emotions this boldly because as compulsive eaters we've built walls around our feelings. It may take a few meetings to get comfortable, but gradually we feel free enough to share.

Telephone Calls

Attending a support group gives us a list of potential friends to call on the telephone when we're overwhelmed with feelings and tempted to overeat. It takes so much humility to call someone that I sometimes still fight it for hours. I have to abandon my individualistic Lone Ranger spirit and my "looking-good kid" image and pick up the telephone and say, "Do you have a few minutes? I need to talk."

Therapy

Professional counselors are trained to help people discover buried emotions and express them in legitimate ways. If you have difficulty expressing yourself or trusting people, you might benefit from a one-on-one relationship with someone who is legally bound to confidentiality.

If you're in a crisis in which you're alienating your spouse and your employer, a therapist may help you monitor and manage rage. Therapists can also help in a crisis because they recognize deeply buried hurts, true suicidal intentions, personality disorders, and physical disorders.

Many compulsives find that investing the time and money in therapy makes them more accountable and keeps them from denying that they have a problem. Be sure to choose a therapist who understands your problem—one who is a recovering compulsive eater and who regularly counsels compulsive eaters.

You may wonder, Can't I get counsel from some godly people or my pastor? That depends on how much that person understands about compulsive behavior. Otherwise, she or he may offer you the "just say no" answer, which works well in preventing compulsive behavior but not so well in overcoming it.

Journaling

In journaling, our pen becomes our instrument of grief, rage, and confusion, and we sort out our thoughts and feelings this way rather than venting them on the people around us. It's as if anger is transferred through our pen as we write the unthinkable things we're thinking.

I didn't plan it this way, but I've written my own journal as a prayer. As I spill my feelings, I address God directly. Sometimes I reread a paragraph and find I've been mean as I've rehearsed why I should tell someone off. Then I usually correct it, and I like setting the record straight.

Art

I don't draw well, so I was surprised at how much it helped me to draw a picture of my eating disorder (as mentioned in Chapter 4). No one else would have recognized that my drawing was an empty house with pillars and no walls, but I knew, and that was enough.

Darlene, who is artistic, expresses her feelings with paints, charcoal, watercolors, and even clay. One time she chose a black crayon and doodled, not necessarily drawing objects. Her therapist pointed out hidden expressions of anger in the scribbling: the door frame and doorknob of the closet in which her father locked her as a child; the engagement ring from a broken relationship. "I got in touch with feelings I'd been avoiding for a long time and worked through them," she says.

Gentle Confrontation

As compulsive eaters, we have lived our life in extremes. In our people-pleasing mode, we didn't confront those who were unfair to us. If our spouse ignored us or flirted with others, we pretended not to notice or made snide remarks. In our "king baby" or "fixer" mode, we may have confronted people so many times that we made enemies of them.

After we've gained clarity through some abstinence and recovery, we can attempt to express our dislike of the way people treat us without being harsh and sarcastic. We can tell them how we feel, using "I" messages, owning our feelings and saying how we would prefer to be treated. We don't invoke pity; we don't shame the person or play "one up"; we don't even demand a response. Our goal is to express our feelings and give our position, not to control the other person.

Confrontation is not necessarily "safe" because we will probably be challenged. It may also be unsafe for us because we have to be careful that we're not acting out of unhealthy desires to fix or control.

LIVING IN OUR FEELINGS

Sometimes we experience our emotions so intensely that it scares us. "Some compulsives see feelings as an indiscriminate black cloud that hovers over them saying, 'Who am I going to get today?'" says psychologist Dr. Peter Robbins of Turning Point Counseling. "It's as if feelings grab them by the throat, throw them to the ground, and move on. They wonder—when will the next depression strike?"[5]

Some become "stuck" in anger or despair. When we live in our feelings or become stuck, nothing else matters because our character defects are running the show. We constantly tune in to our emotions. If we feel depressed, don't tell us your good news because we can't share your joy with you.

We can try to get behind the emotion, however. That's the next step in our stop-look-and-listen inventory. After asking ourselves, How do I *feel?* we ask, What do I *think?* Is a myth or character defect behind this feeling? What is the truth in this situation?

You May Be Wondering . . .

Q Can't I talk to my family and friends about my feelings?

A If they're wrapped up in overeating, thinness, or stifling feelings, they usually don't understand. If you decide to try, choose someone who is a feeling-oriented listener and "share with a teaspoon, not a shovel," says psychologist Dr. Louis Stoetzer of the Adult

Children's Center. "Take three minutes and then change the subject. It's easy to think that you have to share all your feelings, but that can burden others and embarrass yourself."[6]

Oddly enough, a spouse may not be the ideal person with whom to process feelings, cautions Stoetzer. "Typically, people in recovery frighten their spouses with their negative emotions so that it's difficult for spouses to listen. Especially in the beginning, spouses want to fix us."

A counselor suggested that I condense what I said in support group to three sentences and share that with my husband after each meeting. That way my husband knew what I was going through, but I wasn't expecting him to act as my support group. Sometimes he asked questions and we talked about it; other times he didn't.

Q Who should see a therapist?

A "Not everyone could or should be in therapy," says psychologist Dr. Patricia O'Gorman, director of the Adult Child Counseling Center in Albany, New York.

> Therapy is useful for those who want a more insight-oriented approach, who are motivated and want to make an investment in time and money (or who have insurance). Therapy may not be as useful for those who find that recovery programs work for them and are satisfied with that. With all the books, support groups, and conferences available, not everyone needs it, but some people want to work through it in a more individual fashion. Therapy may be useful for the blanks that occur.[7]

If you try therapy, give it a chance to work. Like recovery, therapy can make you feel worse before you feel better. It may take a while to establish a relationship with a therapist, just as it does with a support group.

TEN

Telling Myself the Truth

Have you ever felt this way?

- I'm an emotional basket case.
- My emotions seem to have a life of their own.
- I am never going to be a normal person.

These were the self-destructive thoughts that used to beat me up. They were so powerful that I felt forced to overeat to anesthetize myself. I still put on a happy face, but behind that smile, the picture of my future got more blurred and my guilt bludgeoned all traces of hope within me.

At support groups, others who were as riddled with emotional confusion as I was confessed their shadowy feelings and then compared them with the clear light of reality. That was the step I was missing. I wanted to do that, too.

One of the reasons they could do this so easily was that they had taken their inventories and knew their character defects. These defects pointed them to deeply rooted myths about themselves that drove their compulsive eating. I began trying to find my deeply rooted myths when I took my stop-look-and-listen inventories.

One day I was feeling low because I felt that my husband, Greg, paid no attention to me. He was watching a football game on television and reading the newspaper. I felt like leaving the house and stopping at every taco stand in town, but I was in recovery so I couldn't do that anymore.

Instead I went out on the porch to think, and that's where I fell over my son's skates and yelled as I fell. Greg didn't come out to see what was wrong.

I went into the house, but Greg didn't even look up from his newspaper to notice. I got madder.

I retreated to my room, and I wrote in my journal about how sad and lonely I felt. Yes, I wrote, this is my character defect of self-pity in full bloom, and I want to eat because of it. I doodled in the margin for a minute, trying to figure out what tainted core belief or myth drove me to such self-pity. It sounded terribly maudlin, but I wrote, "Nobody loves me." That was exactly how I felt.

Then I asked myself this important question: What's the truth in this situation?

Now that I had released my emotions, I was calmer. I wrote about how Greg was loyal to me. He had stuck with me in my most critical "king baby" years. Yes, he was presently distracted by the television, but he needed to relax, too. At other times, he did pay attention to me. Each night we talked a lot after the kids went to bed. We had a regular weekly date that was fun. I wrote all these things down.

I felt an urging to be even more rigorously honest, so I wrote, "OK, OK, I faked it with the skates. I just barely tripped over them and made it look like I fell."

I paused and thought, What character defect is operating here?

I painfully admitted that sometimes I tried to get reactions from people by making them feel sorry for me. I paused for a moment to let the humiliation of that admission sink in, and then I asked myself why I did this.

I thought for a while and wrote, "I think I do this because I am always so competent that no one ever gives me sympathy. It's the supposedly incompetent people who get a lot of attention. Sometimes I am so hungry for love and attention that I am willing to do outrageous things to get it."

I thought about how this dysfunctional scheme didn't work very well because Greg, perhaps on a subconscious level, saw through it and didn't respect me for it. At other times I had warned myself to stop it before other people caught on because then they wouldn't like me and that would defeat my purpose: to be loved!

That's what all this was about: not feeling loved. So, I was back to the same myth: Nobody loves me. Then I asked myself one of the most important questions of recovery: What am I going to do about it?

For me, there is only one source of love that won't fail me: God's love. I've been disappointed many times because I've wanted that unconditional love from other human beings, but they have not been equipped to give it. Now I look only to God to fill the holes in my heart so quivering with neediness.

So I prayed for a few minutes and skimmed through a few of my favorite Psalms. Then I reflected for a few minutes on how much God loves me, how he delights in me: "He brought me out into a spacious place; he rescued me because he *delighted* in me" (Ps. 18:19). Yes, he delights in me.

I felt so elated at having followed this sane path that I called my sponsor and reported my progress. Then I sat down next to Greg, who was still watching his game. "Are you enjoying the game?" I asked.

He told me how his team was losing and he was frustrated.

"I was frustrated, too," I said, "because I felt ignored." Greg looked at me and said, "OK. Why don't we take a walk in a half hour?"

That was just what I wanted. I got my needs met because I expressed my needs and feelings in a calm manner without blaming or exaggerating. Before my recovery, I would have acted on all that self-pity (which might have turned to rage) by storming out of the house or creating a verbal war. Through recovery, I was learning how to get my needs met in reasonable and healthy ways.

Even though this situation turned out well, the process was painful, and it always is. Who wants to admit they have such childish attitudes? We can't, unless we focus on how knowing the truth sets us free (John 8:32). A friend of mine has a poster that pictures a limp rag doll with these words printed below her helpless figure: "The truth will make you free, but first it will make you miserable." It's painful to scrutinize your soul this way, but it frees you to consider yourself as you really are and find healing.

Facing the truth involves asking these hard questions:

- How do I *feel* (discussed in Chapter 9)?
- What do I *think?* Is a myth or character defect behind this feeling? What is the truth in this situation?

Eventually we ask, What will I *do?* What tools am I going to use to recover the truth? What am I going to do to avoid sabotaging my recovery?

My small victories facing the truth and asking these questions have convinced me to confront the myths I believe and work through them.

THE MYTHS THAT DRIVE US

The myths or false notions about ourselves, about life, and about God inflame our preoccupation with eating. These myths become "traffic" in our heads that distracts us and turns us into people we don't want to be. These myths become clearer as we move into abstinence because overeating isn't altering our moods. As we gradually clear away this traffic in our heads, we can hear the voice of God more clearly. We can also look into the hearts of our spouse and children and can sense the pure, God-given drives that are within us.

As we pinpoint these myths, we see how distorted they are, and we figure out the corresponding truths. Believing and integrating these truths can be difficult. It helps to talk about them at support groups and read books about particular myths. At some point, we may need to examine the origin of our myths so we can see how distorted they are.

Each time we return to our mythical thinking, we correct it with the truth before it starts the traffic in our heads. This mental dialogue between our myths and the truth may go on for years. We didn't come by these myths easily or quickly, and they will not be changed easily or quickly.

Some of the myths I've heard most often are listed below. They may sound childish because we developed them from our point of view as children. Some of them sound outrageous or heretical, but they express what people believe in their deepest selves. We would probably be too ashamed to say most of them out loud, yet they play like tapes in our minds.

After each myth, I've listed a character defect or unhealthy behavior in parentheses and the corresponding truth on the next line. Below that, I've provided appropriate Scripture on which to meditate to incorporate these truths into your heart.

Myths About Myself

Myth: I am an unimportant, inadequate person (low self-esteem, beating myself up).

Truth: Sometimes I do and say inadequate things, but I am still a valued child of God. Christ thought I was important enough that he died for me. Being valued doesn't mean that I always enjoy being me, because everyone struggles. As I surrender to God, he fills the emptiness of my lack of sense of self that a spouse, relative, or friend cannot fill.

For meditation: Isaiah 64:8; Psalm 95:6–7.

Myth: I am a weak, useless person (laziness, being ruled by others' judgments).

Truth: I am as competent and empowered as I let God enable me to become in spite of what negative relatives and friends may have told me. Besides, God specializes in using the most unlikely candidates, including murderers (Moses, the apostle Paul), adulterers (David), and liars (the apostle Peter).

For meditation: Philippians 1:6, 4:13.

Myth: Because I'm an inadequate person, others usually reject me in personal and job situations (hopelessness).

Truth: When others reject me, it isn't always personal; sometimes it's just the way things happen. When it is personal, people reject us because of their own inadequacies or family history as much as our inadequacies. The most important being of all loves and accepts us and is planning a place of permanent acceptance and rejoicing.

For meditation: Jeremiah 17:7–8; Romans 5:1–5.

Myth: I am not a sexual person (dismissing my sexuality in its proper place).

Truth: Sexuality is a good and right part of ourselves that God created. My sexuality is not erased by being overweight or lacking what our culture says is masculinity or femininity. A wholesome and cherished sex life is possible between spouses who communicate their needs well and genuinely care for each other.

For meditation: Song of Songs 4:1–7, 7:1–13; Proverbs 5:18 (substitute "spouse" for "wife").

Myths About Looking Good

Myth: Do it right! Don't be a failure! It's all or nothing—halfway doesn't count! If I've slipped and eaten popcorn, I might as well eat an entire cheesecake (perfectionism).

Truth: I value progress, not perfection, which is why mistakes are normal, not deadly. My mistakes are even instructive at times. I understand that in life things will go wrong no matter how carefully I plan. Setting goals far beyond my reach sets me up for feeling like a failure, so I don't do that anymore. Being hard on myself doesn't motivate me to do better; it produces guilt and feeds the addictive cycle. It's not wrong to show mercy to myself the way God shows it to me. As I become more flexible and "lighten up," I'll be able to show more love to others.

For meditation: Psalm 103:13–14; Philippians 3:13–14.

Myth: I will never be attractive. I have no right to look pretty/handsome. Looking in the mirror makes me want to overeat (self-loathing, inattention to grooming and appearance).

Truth: Being concerned about appearance is wrong only when I give it a higher priority than it merits. My love for God, my inner life, my relationships will always be more important. Doing the best with the appearance God gave me becomes a natural celebration of my recovery.

For meditation: Psalm 139:13–16; James 1:17–18.

Myth: If I'm in pain, I must be weak or doing something wrong. I have to feel good now (lack of endurance and patience).

Truth: It is normal to go through crises and to feel pain. I learn and grow as I experience pain. It's a sign of strength to live with pain and grow.

For meditation: Hebrews 5:8, 12:11.

Myth: I think I should always be doing something (compulsive busyness to produce self-worth, emphasizing "doing" over "being").

Truth: God values me no matter how much or how little I achieve. Moderation is more acceptable and healthy than overachieving. Who wants to live in a perfectly clean house, anyway? God wants me to learn what it means to rest in his presence and to enjoy him.

For meditation: Exodus 33:14; Haggai 1:5–6.

Myth: I can feel good about myself only if I acquire money, fame, or power (materialism, self-centeredness, controlling).

Truth: God gives me what I need. My culture screams at me that I need these highly addictive items, but even if I acquire them, I will find they're not enough. As I grow in Christ, I learn that fullness in him, not having the perfect career and perfect body with the perfect house in the best neighborhood with perfect children, is my goal.

For meditation: Ecclesiastes 4:8; Matthew 6:19–21.

Myth: I can feel good about myself only if I am thin. It doesn't matter if I'm talented and smart, because if I'm overweight, I'm a failure (being obsessed about thinness).

Truth: I'm within God's will if I eat nutritious meals, exercise regularly, get enough rest, and do not overeat compulsively. If my weight is within the doctor's recommendations, I can be content with it. Being pencil thin will not make me more popular or happy. I refuse to be compulsive about eating—or about looking good.

For meditation: 1 Samuel 16:7; 1 Corinthians 6:19–20.

Myths About the Way the World Works

Myth: There is a diet that will make weight loss easy (magical thinking).

Opposite myth: I can eat all I want and not gain weight (magical thinking).

Truth: I can maintain a proper weight by balanced eating and exercise. I ignore the magical thinking in commercials for "incredible" weight loss techniques and their pictures of extremely thin people eating doughnuts and French fries.

For meditation: Galatians 6:7–9; James 1:23–25.

Myth: The worst usually happens to me. Life will never get better (negative thinking, expecting the worst).

Truth: Bad things do happen, but no one is picking on me or out to get me. Life on earth is not easy or soft for anyone, but I can be one of those people who view it through the lens of gratefulness to God.

For meditation: Jeremiah 29:11; Philippians 4:19.

Myths About How I Relate to Others

Myth: Others have hurt me, so I can depend on only myself (overdependence on others).

Truth: Sometimes others will help me tremendously, but at other times they do not have the emotional or financial resources necessary. I have ended my search for the all-caring parent in my best friend, spouse, pastor, or priest. I know that I will ultimately lose every relationship in my life except my relationship with Christ. He has promised never to leave us, and he's the only one who can keep that promise.

For meditation: John 14:18; Galatians 6:2.

Myth: Asking for help is weak (pride).

Truth: Sharing my struggles with those whom I trust shows strength of character. I have accepted myself as I am, and I trust that sharing my struggles will help others as well as myself. I have given up my looking-good kid image.

For meditation: Proverbs 27:17; Paul's example of sharing his weaknesses in Romans 7:14–15.

Myths: I'm worthy only until someone worthier comes along (jealousy). If everyone was created equal, I should have what others have (greed).

Truth: God gives me the attention and material things I need. I trust that God blesses each person, including me, as he sees fit. This gratefulness helps me see that even if I live in a one-room apartment, I'm "rich" compared to most of the people on this planet.

For meditation: Philippians 2:13; 1 Thessalonians 5:18.

Myth: My life is harder than other people's lives (self-pity).

Truth: God doesn't allow me to experience struggles that are too difficult for me. He gives me the grace I need for each struggle. Since people are secretive about struggles, I can't make comparisons.

For meditation: 1 Corinthians 10:13; Hebrews 12:10–11.

Myths About God

The great scheme of the enemy is to distort our relationship with God so that we are miserable and needy, requiring compulsive behaviors to cope.

Myth: God doesn't love me (projecting others' views and treatment of me to God).

Truth: God loves me with an overwhelming, extravagant love. Even if I'm the only person struggling, God seeks me relentlessly as the shepherd left the ninety-nine to seek the one lost sheep (Luke 15:3–7). God doesn't wait around for me to love him, rather he pursues me relentlessly to establish a meaningful relationship with me. Says Quaker author and teacher Douglas Steere, "God holds me and every other son and daughter of Adam in a longing gaze, seeking to wake each of us out of our drowse of preoccupation and self-absorption that we might realize who it is that loves us.[1]

For meditation: Romans 8:35–39; 1 John 3:1.

Myth: God loves me more when I am good, when I work hard for him (projecting the perfectionism of others on to God).

Truth: God loves me unconditionally. He isn't like Santa Claus, who brings gifts to only the good boys and girls. He is like the father in the parable of the prodigal son (Luke 15:11–32). I can imagine the father standing on the porch waiting so he could see the boy while he was still far away (Luke 15:20b). I can see the father running down the trail to embrace the boy, just as God runs to me, embraces me, and forgives me.

Being worthy of God's love is not only impossible, it's beside the point. The Christian life is not about being worthy of God but about surrendering to him.

For meditation: 1 John 4:10; Romans 5:8.

A CONTINUAL PROCESS

This internal mental dialogue between the myths we're giving up and the truths we're absorbing occurs many times a day. Just when you think you've dismantled a myth, an event can occur that makes you learn it again from a different angle. Becky was working on her recovery and had a month or so of abstinence when she found out her husband was being transferred to another part of the country. They were thrilled because they had wanted to change locations anyway, and they knew they could buy a better home there.

But a strange agony set in. Becky started eating. What was wrong?

Becky asked herself the questions of these last two chapters. First, she examined her feelings and found she felt worthless and fat. In the midst of this, her brother commented, "This is no big deal. You've moved before."

Then Becky thought about how, eight years before, she'd moved across the country with her former husband, who often abused her, saying, "You're a fat cow!" (She'd weighed only 110 pounds.) He kept comparing her to women in his skin magazines. He even rejected her sexually. Becky had put the horror of this relationship behind her and never mentioned her former husband's name.

Becky examined the truth of the situation, which was that she was now a successful careerwoman, wife, and mother. She now understood her worth in God's eyes. No character defect was operating here except that she was believing one of her old myths of worthlessness.

What did Becky do about it? She went to her recovery group and talked about it. There she confessed her disgust toward her former husband. She also stated the truth that the person he had talked about was not her but someone he tried to make her. "This time is different," she told the group. "I'm making a wise move with a husband who truly loves me. This is a good move."

As each event occurs, we search our feelings and redirect the traffic in our heads until it falls in line with what is true about ourselves, others, the world, and God.

We soak in these truths daily, because our myths will try to haunt us for years. It doesn't matter so much that our progress is slow, as long as it's steady. When you get impatient, think about this comparison.

> The nature of water is soft, that of stone is hard; but if a bottle is hung above the stone, allowing the water to fall drop by drop, it wears away the stone. So it is with the word of God; it is soft and our heart is hard, but the [person] who hears the word of God often opens his [or her] heart to the fear of God.[2]

Q Aren't you saying that if I think good thoughts I'll be OK?

A No. I have purposely not used the phrase "reprogramming your mind," because it is not that simple. Too many people hyperspiritualize this process, as if you can pray away these myths in an afternoon. People who claim to do this are often repressing their emotions, which, if they're compulsive eaters, creates a need to eat compulsively.

Renewing the mind is possible, though. Each time a myth presents itself to our minds, we answer back with a truth. These mental dialogues occur over and over until they permeate every layer of our self—spiritual, psychological, and physical. We meditate on and journal about these truths. Slowly the truth becomes more real to us, and the chaotic traffic in our head quiets down. Eventually the myths leave us.

ELEVEN

What's Behind the Myths?

Several centuries ago scientists formulated a theory called spontaneous generation—that living matter sprang from nonliving matter. Scientists postulated, for example, that the juices of decaying meat produced maggots. In the 1600s, a biologist disproved this theory by showing that maggots did not breed in meat when flies were kept from laying eggs in it. He showed that complex creatures were reproduced only by others like themselves.

The emotional neediness of compulsive eaters does not spontaneously generate, either. Our neediness usually develops within our family of origin because our family is dysfunctional in some way. For example, Barbara McFarland and Tyeis Baker-Baumann, who direct and coordinate teams, respectively, at the Eating Disorders Recovery Center in Cincinnati, Ohio, write in their book *Feeding the Empty Heart* that children who grow up in families in which one or both parents are alcoholic are prone to develop eating disorders.[1]

Professionals and compulsives alike are discovering that some degree of neediness exists in families with all kinds of dysfunctions. These dysfunctions might be seemingly benign ones, such as overeating, controlling, or focusing all their attention on a family member who is ill. No doubt some of the neediness we feel as compulsive eaters springs from our dysfunctional family background.

But my family wasn't dysfunctional, you may protest. Nearly all families are dysfunctional to some extent.[2] In a book I coauthored with therapist Curt Grayson, *Creating a Safe Place,* we explain that a dysfunctional family is simply one in which children do not get the love and attention they need.[3] A dysfunctional family is like a dry sponge. It lacks enough moisture or flexibility or even bulk to be used to wipe off a counter. In the same way, some families lack the necessary nurturing or flexibility or structure to raise children with healthy self-esteem. Children in these families often turn to compulsive behavior to feel loved.

The dysfunctional (or codependent) family system is described by McFarland and Baker-Baumann as

> a dysfunctional, non-equal relationship between spouses, who both may have low self-esteem. Spouses look to others to get needs met, often without knowing what their needs are and without directly discussing their needs. Since they're unable to meet their own needs they're unable to meet the needs of their children.[4]

While some children are resilient, others are not. They copy their parents' patterns of low self-esteem and inability to communicate needs. To compensate, these children take drugs or binge, purge, or starve themselves. Still other children seem to move through childhood unscathed only to find that as adults they cannot cope with life unless they're eating compulsively.

A TRIGGERING EVENT?

As the jungle of the dysfunctional family creates a breeding ground for compulsive eating, specific events can occur to spark that need. Psychologist Dr. Louis Stoetzer has found that while men cannot usually pinpoint when their addiction began, women often can. It's usually a traumatic event in their lives—for example, a boy jilts them in high school, their parents divorce, they don't get to finish college.[5]

In some dysfunctional families, the triggering event for children is sexual abuse.[6] Barbara McFarland says that 65 to 70 percent of the patients at the Eating Disorders Recovery Center were sexually abused. Jan Frank, therapist and author of *A Door of Hope,* has found that 95 percent of the obese people she has worked with were sexually abused as children.[7]

"They were often made to feel responsible for their abuse by the abuser's comments that they were so cute or attractive, sexy, or lovable," says Frank. "They internalized this message in their subconscious mind and decided to protect themselves by being overweight or unattractive. If they do start to lose weight and receive attention from men, it scares them to death. In order to cope, they often respond by gaining fifty more pounds than they originally lost."

Sexual abuse can be subtle, too. Therapist Charlene Underhill notes that some of her clients who are compulsive eaters were not molested but saw a parent walking around naked and felt the inappropriateness of it. "Even accidental exposure to nakedness, in which parents say, 'Oh, I didn't know you were here,' can cause people to react by covering themselves up with extra pounds."[8]

Other times sexual abuse was subtle because it was communicated only in words. Parents made inappropriate or suggestive comments that resulted in the children feeling shamed and needing to insulate themselves with excess weight.

Some women who are compulsive eaters but who were not abused have a victim perspective because they were oppressed as women. "They were made to feel they couldn't achieve because they were women," says Underhill. "Now they use extra pounds to say, 'I want you to love me for myself, so I'm going to be fat.' Overeating becomes a way to revictimize themselves."

Issues such as these create and cement in our minds myths such as those listed in the last chapter. Dismantling these myths often requires that we investigate the patterns of our own dysfunctional family of origin. Then we understand our myths better, which can empower us to choose not to believe them anymore.

THE DYSFUNCTIONAL FAMILY AND ITS MYTHS

Several of the unhealthy patterns of the dysfunctional family generate myths in compulsive overeaters as children. (The characteristics of these families are named in detail in other works and provide helpful reading.) Here are a few of the most common patterns and the myths to which they give rise.

Inappropriately Expressed Feelings

"When there was distress in [dysfunctional] families," says psychiatrist Dr. Edward Khantzian, "people didn't hold each other through that discomfort and say, 'I'm sorry you felt that way. Come over and sit by me, and I will be with your distress.' The methods of the dysfunctional family are: Keep it to yourself and stuff it. Or they don't even acknowledge the distress, or they go out and get in a frenzy-oriented activity."[9]

In some families, feelings were overexpressed in a dramatic way. Family members didn't have headaches, they were dying. Problems were solved only after days of the silent treatment and then a major showdown. No holiday was complete without a dramatic exit, reentrance, and tearful reunion. The parent who told you that you would never amount to anything later said what a wonderful kid you were.

Myths: If I'm a "nice" or "good" person, I won't talk about my hurt—I won't even feel it. Or: I will make a big deal out of every hurt.

Truth: I can get my emotional needs met by expressing my feelings in appropriate ways.

For meditation: Psalm 56:8; Mark 3:5.

Violated Boundaries

If parents in dysfunctional families tried to control their children, the children may have grown up to find that they can't distinguish between their desires and others' desires. They become people pleasers to survive emotionally. When they ask themselves as adults why they do what they do, the answer revolves around not upsetting someone or trying to make someone happy. Their decisions often have little to do with their needs, strengths, and abilities. As a result, their needs don't get met, and they use coping mechanisms such as eating compulsively.

Other times family members did not own their own guilt, and they violated children's boundaries by putting their guilt on the children. As adults, they may feel as if everything is their fault. If their spouse was fired from his or her job, it's somehow their fault! If their friend gets mad, they feel they must have ruined the relationship.

Sexual abuse victims may have a difficult time setting sexual boundaries because their own boundaries were so violated in childhood. They may develop no boundaries, becoming promiscuous, or they may build cement boundaries so that they strangle the sex life of their marriage.

Myths: I must please others to be happy. Everything that happens is my fault. I must either express my sexuality in an unhealthy way or repress it.

Truths: I please God as I think he wants me to please him. I take responsibility for those things that are my fault but nothing more. I strive to express my sexuality according to godly guidelines.

For meditation: Galatians 1:10; 1 Thessalonians 2:4–6.

Enmeshment

Children become enmeshed with parents when their relationship is so close that their identities and self-worth become entangled. This happens most often between mothers and daughters, as daughters feel they have to take care of their mothers and tell their mothers all their secrets. To hold anything back feels dishonest.

Enmeshment with parents distorts the adult child's marital relationship because he or she is "married" in a sense to the parent. Or the adult child may become enmeshed with the spouse or their children instead of letting those family members have their own identities.

Myth: My life is built around a certain person (parent, spouse, child).

Truths: I am my own separate person who allows God to fill my empty places. Loving others means I can let them be their own persons and that I don't depend on them to meet my deepest needs.

For meditation: Luke 2:48–49; John 2:3–5.

Tension

The drama, judgment, and inconsistency in the dysfunctional family meant that life was not predictable for children. They may have felt nervous about what would happen next and who it would happen to. Nobody laughed at mistakes. These children may have carried that tension into their school settings and relationships and even isolated themselves. Then they wondered why they were lonely.

As adults, they take themselves too seriously and have difficulty having fun in the sense of letting go. If in their childhood they feared chaos in their families, they may become hooked on controlling their environment. They control schedules, their possessions, their family members. They want to know what's happening at all times, who's in charge, and how they can voice their opinion about it.

Myths: I must never embarrass myself. I must control each detail to keep more bad things from happening.

Truths: I can laugh at myself. I can go with the flow of life and trust that if things don't work out, I will cope anyway.

For meditation: Proverbs 19:21, 31:25.

Unworthiness

These families may have communicated the feeling that nobody deserves anything or that some people deserve everything and others deserve nothing. "When my mom rewarded me for doing something right," says Maggie, "she gave me food, but then she talked about how fattening it was, so I didn't enjoy it."

Myth: I deserve nothing.

Truth: I feel thankful and glad when others notice my achievements. If others overlook my accomplishments, I can reward myself in healthy ways.

For meditation: Mark 10:13–16; James 1:17–18.

Role Reversal

Many times children were expected to parent the parents and other children in the house. Children offered emotional comfort and even assisted parents with chores in a way not usually expected of children. Children thought, *I am the child, but I have the power to keep my parents together. My parents need me to comfort and encourage them, thus I am really the parent.*

This sometimes results in feelings of grandiosity—I solved my parents' problems as a mere child, just think what I can do as an adult!

Myth: I must take care of my parent—and everyone else as well.

Truth: I am responsible for myself. God may lead me to help others, but I cannot solve their problems for them.

For meditation: Exodus 20:12 (Does it *honor* parents to parent them?); 2 Corinthians 12:14.

If these myths are deeply rooted in our thought patterns, it will take time to work through them, but it's worth it. When not addressed, they can create guilt and depression that hang on us like a soaked winter coat and drag us down. They create in us an inordinate need for comfort and, therefore, a great need to overeat.

Food Talks Back

Even as children, we knew something was not right about the dysfunctional tendencies of our families. We longed to change things, but we were powerless figures in the family, so we began using food to talk back to our families. Here are some of the things we learned to say with food.

I Can Make Myself Feel Better We rewarded ourselves and rebuilt our flagging self-esteem with food. "Compulsive eating provides a mood alteration," says therapist Jan Frank. "You become addicted to the feeling of eating twenty-five cookies."[10]

I Can Cope When we were asked to be the parent or forced to listen to endless arguing, we coped by eating. It numbed the feelings, and we didn't have to think about how much we hurt.

I'll Show You! We may have used our overeating as a way to secretly rebel, saying, "I am perfect enough!" or to take revenge on parents, saying, "I am as good as my supposedly perfect older brother!"

I Can Soothe My Anger When we imitated our "king baby" parent by expressing our anger, we were told that we shouldn't act that way. It wasn't nice to be angry. We learned to suppress and even swallow our anger by overeating.

I Can Feel Loved If our parents gave us food as expressions of their love for us, we still feel loved when we eat. "Food is mother," says Jan Frank. "Compulsive eating often makes up for a lack of nurturing and bonding and provides a temporary source of comfort."

Now, as adults, we still seek nurturing, especially if we spend a lot of time nurturing others. Food becomes a convenient way to do that.

I Can Depend on Something We may never have known what was going to happen in our families, but we could count on the French fries at McDonald's to be skinny, salty, and tasty. We created our stashes of junk food so that we could always have something we could count on—something with the same flavor, shape, and texture to be there when we needed it.

I Will Build My Own World We may have wanted to escape what was going on because we didn't understand it and it was painful. When we sat down to eat macaroni and cheese, we entered another world for a few minutes. It was a dreamland, of sorts, and we didn't have to deal with anybody. It separated us from all that we didn't understand, and we felt at peace in our world.

I Can Punish Myself We felt ugly, useless, and dumb, so we felt as if we might as well eat. Yes, we would gain weight, but we deserved it. We may have even used our diets as a regulated way to beat ourselves up.

I Will Protect Myself Children who were sexually abused were often told by the perpetrators that the abuse was their fault because they asked for it in some way. Extra pounds and baggy clothing became a shield of protection so future perpetrators would keep their distance.

I Will Fit In Some parents laid down the family rules in so many words: "You'll have big thighs and hips like your mother, grandmother, and all the women in our family," and we felt obliged to fit in. Other times, it was unspoken, but we loved (and desperately needed) these adults so much that we eventually gained the weight to fit in. To have healthy eating habits would have been an indictment of their being overweight.

Tandem Recovery?

Recovery from compulsive eating and from dysfunctional family issues can help each other. When you work on your abstinence, old feelings come up, so you explore your character defects and myths and find their roots in your childhood dysfunctional family. As you work through these myths, you feel uncomfortable and consider overeating to deny the pain, but your abstinence helps you face those issues with clarity.

But which recovery should I work on first? people ask. "Each recovery has to come when it comes," says Barbara McFarland, whose book *Feeding the Empty Heart* deals with recovery from both compulsive eating and dysfunctional family issues. "I don't think you can isolate issues and say, 'I'm going to deal with this first, and then I'm going to deal with that.' You have to go with the flow of your own recovery."[11]

If a compulsive eater finds that recovery doesn't seem to work for them or that they regain their weight, they might consider working through childhood sexual abuse issues. Facing such issues as false guilt and loss of trust can make them feel safe enough to abandon the protectors that weight and eating have become.

"I tell a patient who is a compulsive eater and who has been sexually abused," says McFarland, "that it's important for them to deal with the sexual abuse at some point. I ask them if they're ready, but if their energy isn't there, then we can't force it."

Yet others may accuse them of forcing the issue because it's not unusual for memories of childhood sexual abuse to be vague. "People worry that they're making up their abuse because their memories of it are unclear," says Jan Frank. "Yet when you consider that one in three women and one in five men have been sexually abused by the time they're eighteen, it may not be that unlikely."[12]

You May Be Wondering . . .

Q What's to stop people from blaming their problems on their parents?

A Parents aren't scapegoats, because recovery is about taking responsibility, not about judging others. Some of our problems may be rooted in the dysfunctionality of our family, but it is our problem now. Even when sexual abuse victims confront their perpetrators, that doesn't alleviate their need and personal responsibility to look at how they interact with people.

Besides, blame is difficult to assess. "Addicts are often children of addicts who themselves were never treated," says psychologist Dr. Patrick Carnes. "Counselors find themselves treating three and four generations of the same family. If it were a question of punishment, you'd have to decide which generation to punish."[13]

Besides, the need to place blame is typical of "all-or-nothing thinking," which we are giving up. Our families were neither perfect nor terrible. All families have some problems.

Deciding who to blame is also typical of the grandiosity that says we know what everyone is thinking and so have the right to judge them. We didn't know all the facts then, and we probably don't know them now. If our parents were compulsive in some way (overeating, alcoholism, controlling), they have often been acting out of their compulsion, not their true feelings for us. Recovery means that we give people a break. We realize that our family members coped the best they could, just as we are doing.

Q How do I view God as a loving parent if my parents were harsh or abusive?

A It's possible to view God as the parent you've needed and searched for. One way to do this is to study and meditate on

God's character as a parent, especially as he is symbolized in parables.

The searching woman (Luke 15:8–10): God is symbolized by a woman who searched into the night for a tiny coin lost in the straw floor of her Palestinian hut. When she found it, she threw a party! God is patient; he is determined to help us no matter how lost we feel; he loves to celebrate over us.

The accepting father (Luke 15:11–32): God is symbolized by a father who loved his prodigal son no matter how far astray the boy had gone (see "Myths About God" in Chapter 10). This helps us see that God bases his love for us not on our being "good enough" but on the boundless way he loves us as his children.

The eccentric vineyard owner (Matt. 20:1–16): God is symbolized by this seemingly illogical employer who showered a full day's wage on both full-timers and latecomers (some of whom worked only one hour). That sounds like something only a grandmother would do! It helps us see that God loves us not because of what we do but because he chooses to love us.

The unjust judge (Luke 18:1–8): God is symbolized as the opposite of an unjust judge who kept putting off a widow seeking justice. As if to dispel our suspicions that God doesn't love us, Jesus said that God is not like this cantankerous judge; God administers justice quickly for those who cry out day and night.

Another way to appreciate God's love for us is to set aside his parental role and choose one of his other roles: creator, rescuer, caretaker of the animals and the world. Robin feels she can't trust a parent figure, so she focuses on God as her creator. "I am his creation, his beautiful work of art," she says. "Artists don't shame their creations. They take very good care of them, as God takes care of me."

TWELVE

"Solo" Tools of Recovery

"Mom," my son whispered to me. "Why do you keep asking that lady the same thing?"

Since I was talking on the telephone to someone from our eating disorders support group, it took a minute to understand what my son meant.

Then I asked that question again, and I heard it: "So, what are you going to do about it?"

I'd listened to my recovering friend share her feelings. We'd talked about what those feelings indicated about what she believed about herself, but I could see that she was getting stuck in those emotions and didn't want to move out of them. I felt as if she wanted me to wave a magic wand and make her better. I kept tossing the recovery ball back into her lap by asking: What are you going to do about it?

That day I realized that this "do" question was an important part of my stop-look-and-listen inventory.

- How do I *feel?*
- What do I *think?* Is a myth or character defect behind this feeling? What is the truth in this situation?
- What will I *do?* What tools am I going to use to recover the truth? What am I going to do to avoid sabotaging my recovery?

After I knew what I felt, and what I thought, I needed to decide what I would do. The answer to this question is usually one or more of the recovery tools. Using the tools nudges us out of regret or anger or self-judgment. It requires that we turn from our old ways and point ourselves toward recovery.

Some of the tools require that we partner with others, such as attending support group meetings and contacting a sponsor.

Others are done in solo fashion, but their tentacles reach deep within us and show themselves in a bright, steady serenity that others eventually see. Here are some of those solo tools.

LITERATURE

When you're in need of more information about recovery or you want to read about someone else's walk, a recovery book, magazine, or pamphlet can be helpful. Underline the parts you like best, because it's fun to reread the underlined sentences again months later and find strength and hope when you're feeling blue. Sometimes I bring a book with me to a support group meeting. I read the paragraph that was most helpful to me and tell the group how it helped.

Twelve-Step literature is full of pithy slogans that help us on the run. As my son and I put together a stereo cabinet, we both felt frustrated. I couldn't leave him to write in my journal, but I could, and did, say, "Progress, not perfection," many times. We can answer our myths on the spur of the moment with slogans like these:

- One day at a time.
- How important is it?
- This too shall pass.
- Listen and learn.
- If it works, don't fix it.
- First things first.
- Easy does it.
- Turn it over.
- Keep it simple.

- Fake it till you make it.
- Principles before personalities.
- Progress, not perfection.

These slogans reinforce on a daily basis the truths we've committed ourselves to learning.

Recovery may affect all our reading habits. It often opens the mind to new slants on our faith. I had always been "doing" for God, but my recovery made me more interested in "being" with God, so I began reading books and magazines about meditation and knowing God. Some of my recovery friends who were never interested in "doing" issues started reading magazines from world poverty relief organizations. This is a healthy result of our recovery—seeking balance in our spiritual life.

PRAYER

The traffic in our heads can get loud as our character defects block us. Prayer becomes one of our paths to serenity. Madeleine L'Engle describes it this way: "In prayer . . . the mind and the heart, the intellect and the intuition, the conscious and the subconscious mind, stop fighting each other and collaborate."[1]

That collaboration between the different parts of ourselves includes God, now that we've quit running away from what he wants and burying ourselves in food. Now we run to him, using many styles of prayer. I described gut-level prayer earlier as a tool to express feelings. Here are two more kinds of prayer that can be powerful tools in recovery.

Praise and Worship

The more we surrender to God, the more we become aware that God is a great and powerful being. It makes sense to honor him for who he is. Now that I'm throwing off my perfectionism, I relish my humanity, and I want to praise the only one who really does know what's going on. Praising God replaces my grandiosity; worshipping him replaces worshipping food; thanking him replaces my complaining.

We used to celebrate food—now we celebrate God. At first, I didn't know what to say to praise God. Finally, I borrowed the psalmist's expressions of praise, word for word: "His steadfast love endures forever" (Ps. 118:1, RSV). At other times, I launched out into praising God for qualities I admired such as creativity and compassion.

"Constant Contact"

People through the ages have muddled over the idea of praying without ceasing (1 Thess. 5:17, KJV). Perhaps this refers to what Brother Lawrence, a monk who worked in a monastery kitchen, called "practicing the presence of God." In the Twelve Steps, it's called maintaining "conscious contact with God" (mentioned in Step Eleven), and others call it "centering" on God.

A twelfth-century writer, Bernard of Clairvaux, described how this continuous conversation with God helps us work through struggles:

> When I am at rest, I accuse myself of neglecting my work; and when I am at work, of having disturbed my repose. The only remedy in these uncertainties is prayer, entreating to be shown God's holy Will at every moment, that he may tell us what to do and when and how to do it.[2]

This is the kind of prayer that permeates our lives the way blood circulates through the body. We're in and out of it all day. It adequately fills the empty spaces we used to try to stuff with food.

I have always wanted to practice the presence of God, but I found it difficult. Saying the first three steps ("I can't, God can, I'll let him") as I struggled in those first days of abstinence gave me a taste of contacting God all day long.

As my preoccupation has subsided, I've had to work at keeping this continuing contact, but it's easier than before my recovery. Because I commit my abstinence to God every day before I get out of bed, I also remember to greet God then and to invite him to continue his presence in my life throughout the day.

This growing conscious contact with God has given me a sense of gatheredness, or centeredness, that I haven't known before. I recently noticed how often being scattered was a curse to the Israelites in the Old Testament (Gen. 49:5–7). That was the curse of my compulsive eating, too, and my compulsive busyness, and my compulsive Supermom activities. I was always hurried and focused on too many things. I still get that way sometimes, but it feels so wrong that I abandon it quickly. I refused to be a scattered person now that I know what it means to be gathered before God.

The more we pray this way, the less we pray those old manipulative and blaming prayers: "If you love me, please get me out of this jam."

A journal entry from these recovery years reads:

> Put your arms around me, God. Take away the rage inside me. Take away my expectations. Let me concentrate on you and your love. Let me seek your will daily. I need more of you, not more career success, not more of my husband, not more of my kids, not more of my friends, but more of you.

SCRIPTURE READING

In recovery, our listening skills improve, and this helps us understand Scripture better. One friend who previously didn't read Scripture began reading it a lot. He often referred to the phrase "slaves to sin" (Rom. 6:6), and would say, "This describes me perfectly. God understands how I felt about food."

I, who had always majored in the "shoulds" and "thou shalts" of Scripture, found balance as I began searching the Psalms for verses about how God delights in me (Ps. 18:19, 22:8, 35:27, 147:11, 149:4). I found myself quoting and requoting, "While we were still sinners, Christ died for us" (Rom. 5:8). I needed to know that God loved me, and I found many parables and Old Testament examples to prove it to myself. It's as if my friend and I had previously found only parts of God and now we were discovering other parts.

MEDITATION

We picture Scripture in our minds and find its application to our struggles. For example, I often meditate on Psalm 18:4–19, with its dramatic, Cecil B. De Mille–like rescue scene, which I feel pictures the process of my recovery. Before my recovery, the "cords of death entangled me" (verse 4). Then verses 7–15 show how God heard my voice and charged out of the clouds to rescue me as I began attending the support group and finding that its members loved and accepted me. The changes that occurred in my life were not unlike trembling and quaking mountains (verse 7). There were dramatic turnarounds in my behavior as if God "parted the heavens and came down" (verse 9) and "scattered the enemies" (verse 14). Many times I felt as if I were in the grips of my enemy/character defects, and God swooped "down from on high and took hold of me" (verse 16).

Verse 19 describes the result: "He brought me out into a *spacious place*; he rescued me because he delighted in me." I still read it, shut my eyes, and picture each of the events of these verses and then return to reality with a wider sense of my "spacious place" of recovery.

Many times I consider a troublesome situation in my life after I meditate on a passage. Sometimes I even picture myself in the troublesome situation, and it's amazing how having meditated on Scripture helps me know what to do about the situation.

SILENCE

Taking time for solitude each day helps us center ourselves, to quiet down all the traffic in our heads, to set aside our hidden agenda (usually eating or controlling). My mind is usually so full when I begin that I often have to turn each issue over to God, one by one, and then rest in his presence.

For me, a person who had become a Type A personality, being silent for a few minutes was almost as radical as practicing abstinence. But recovery prepared me. Choosing my best goal weight, choosing my own abstinence, and choosing how to write my inventory gave me a new sense of waiting on God and walking in faith.

It takes a few minutes to become comfortable "keeping company with God." This is different from meditation because I'm not focusing on anything except that I am in God's presence. In a relaxed way, I'm understanding that I can be still and know that God is God (Ps. 46:10). I can return to my world free of my neediness for attention.

JOURNALING

We use journaling not only to express feelings that would scare or hurt others but also to record our thoughts and insights. Sometimes I ask questions and find myself answering them in a flash of insight. I believe that God uses my own journal to speak to me.

A journal can also act as a diary—a safe place for secrets that we aren't ready to tell a support group. It's a place to ask the silliest questions that you're sure others would laugh at. One time I wrote: "I love food so much. What will I do if there's no food in heaven? How will I survive? Will it be fun?"

I also record helpful sayings, quotes, and ideas in the back of my journal. When I borrow a book, I may copy a helpful passage from it in the back. Copying it solidifies the ideas in my mind. In some of those empty moments when nothing makes sense, it's fun to read through these back pages and regain some momentum.

Many people say that we should journal once a day or at some regular interval. Part of what my recovery has taught me is to trust myself about my needs. I journal whenever I need to. Sometimes that's several days a week; sometimes that's once a month. I see it as a tool, not as a taskmaster.

Sometimes when I'm feeling blue, I make a "gratitude list" in which I attempt to name everything I'm grateful for in a certain area of my life: family, support group, community, neighborhood, even my bed.

ABSTINENCE

This tool enhances our ability to use the other solo tools, which is encouraging especially for those who find prayer, meditation, and

Scripture reading difficult. Abstinence (or "refusing outward consolations," as the fifteenth-century monk Thomas a Kempis puts it) heightens your spiritual sensitivity: "If you refuse outward consolations, then you will be able to apply your mind to heavenly things, and frequently to experience inward joy."[3]

There's probably some deep spiritual explanation for this, but let's just say that abstinence removes one god and makes room for the real God.

BALANCING THE TOOLS

We compulsive eaters aren't good at balance, and most of us lean on one set of tools or the other. The solo tools, which I can practice privately, come more naturally to an introvert like me, and I have to work at using the ones that involve others. I've always been a strong-willed loner, and it's humiliating to admit that I need other people. As a know-it-all, I always figured out everything for myself. How could I need someone else?

I struggle with understanding that I can't recover by myself. At first, I didn't want to attend meetings or say anything once I got there. I still die a thousand humiliating deaths before I make a telephone call for support. Many times God has done for me what I could not do for myself through someone I have called. Another person's bumbling support helps me stop wanting to eat or it pulls me out of the blues. I'm still amazed when it happens.

My friend Laura is not this way. She loves to go to meetings, and she's good at using recovery tools that involve others. It used to be that when she had a crisis (before recovery, we don't have problems, we have crises), she called five or six people to get consolation. Once when no one was available she told a few of us the next week, "I got so desperate I had to pray."

"So it got that bad!" we teased her. "You had to pray!"

"It worked," Laura laughed. "After I prayed, I called and one of you answered the phone!"

Balance has become one more area of surrender for both of us. We've had to find a stable rhythm between doing our solo recovery work and asking for help, between depending on God alone and depending on the way he works through others.

You May Be Wondering . . .

Q Does using these tools replace daily devotions?

A Praying, meditating, journaling, being silent, and reading Scripture and other devotional literature shape my "quiet time" (or daily devotions). For years, I strained and fumed trying to have a quiet time, and now that I'm interested in "being" with God, "doing" daily devotions has come up behind me and surprised me.

I know there are many formulas for quiet times, but I, the recovering compulsive controller, have abandoned them. I just do it, and it's not perfect. I don't wait for God to speak in some dramatic way. I meet with God to listen, and I consider that I'm hearing him in whatever I'm reading, writing, or praying about.

In one week, I have various kinds of quiet times at different times of the day and of different lengths depending on the days. I've had to abandon that legalistic, black-and-white thinking that insists that I never miss a single day. That attitude would kill my quiet time. When I miss it, I find I'm yearning to sneak it in elsewhere in my day. I don't go with specific expectations in mind other than to meet God in some way.

THIRTEEN

Partnered Tools of Recovery

My first attempt to work a program of recovery was to read a recovery book. I had learned a lot in life by reading books, and I thought could learn recovery that way, too. I knew about support groups, but my life had been so crowded with committee meetings that I felt burned out with meetings. So I tried to work this program the way I lived my life—in emotional isolation. I felt I didn't need any partners in my recovery. I could do it myself.

Only I couldn't do it alone. I became so miserable trying that I visited Overeaters Anonymous meetings here and there with a friend. She kept asking me to go to a certain meeting she'd heard about. I didn't want to go because it was so far away and I didn't want to make that drive at night through congested traffic. Finally, I was so desperate that one night I called her and said, "Either I'm going to that meeting with you, or I'm going to the ice cream parlor. If I go to the ice cream parlor, I'm going to eat ice cream until I'm sick."

She agreed to go with me. At the meeting, I identified so much with what the people said that I made that drive at night in congested traffic for years thereafter.

Recovery requires that we partner with people to break the isolation so common among compulsive overeaters. The recovery tools that require partnering put a dent in the walls of distrust we have erected. They create settings in which we can learn to trust people in healthy ways.

Like the solo tools described in the previous chapter, the partnered tools are slight variations on tools that Christians have been using for centuries. None of the tools are the answer in themselves; they are merely a means to an end—surrendering more of ourselves to God.

SUPPORT GROUP MEETINGS

In these safe places, we not only express feelings but also share our secret eating behaviors, our character defects, and our myths, no matter how disgusting they may seem to us. We hear others share their experience, strength, and hope, and we come to believe that this can happen to us, too. We make ourselves accountable to refocus our behaviors by surrendering them to God and to the group.

What Is a Support Group?

For those who don't understand the Twelve-Step approach to support groups, it's easier to say what they are not. A support group is not a class, although information may be shared. It is not a gripe session, although some people may "air dirty laundry." It is not a therapy group, although we do work through experiences. It is not a healing session, although we do ask God to give us the hope we need so badly. Groups that are sponsored by churches are not Bible studies, although the Bible is the source of truth for these groups. (Overeaters Anonymous functions as a support group. Other recovery networks offer support group meetings for compulsive eaters. See Appendix 3 for more information about specific support groups.)

If you want recovery but you don't want to bother attending a support group, you're normal. We have that grandiosity about us that says we can recover alone. It's so difficult to admit that we need others that simply showing up at a meeting is a powerful step out of denial.

How Can Attending Support Groups Help?

Aren't people who attend support groups losers? If they were experts, if they were overcomers, they wouldn't be there, right? Aren't they pooling their ignorance?

Recovery teaches us that God often uses unlikely people to speak to us. I'm still amazed that I usually learn the most from the person I have chosen not to like or respect. I can't explain this except to say that the Holy Spirit becomes unleashed in this loose band of strugglers who commit themselves to sharing themselves and accepting each other no matter what. Sometimes when a person speaks, I feel as if God is speaking directly to me through that person. That feeling occurs often in support groups because you identify so well with what is said.

After I finally began sharing in the group, I surprised the other members and myself by quoting back to the group wise things the others had said in previous meetings. "When did I say that?" they would ask afterward. "When you were wearing the red shirt and sitting in that corner," I'd tell them. Without intending to help me, they changed the way I looked at myself and fueled my recovery.

Another startling way in which the Holy Spirit speaks to me is through what I say in the group. When I'm sharing my dilemma, I'll suddenly blurt out answers I didn't know I had. Thinking out loud in a support group lets me discover answers for myself, and I don't forget them that way.

A support group functions ideally as a place of unconditional acceptance. Liz, who was bulimic, was a highly respected church leader and was riddled with guilt. Her despair propelled her through the addictive cycle several times a day. After she broke three weeks of abstinence, she came to the group and shared the shame she felt.

As Liz talked, we listened and smiled. After the meeting, one of us reflected, "But Liz, you have three weeks of your life that you've taken care of yourself, and those three weeks count."

Liz looked far away that night, as if she were could barely taste and feel the affirmation she was being offered.

Months after that, Liz told us that breaking her abstinence and not being shamed by others changed her and gave her hope. "That night was the first time I saw any possibility that I could be free," she said.

Like Liz, I have beaten myself up most of my life. It doesn't help; it only wears me out. I know that if I blow my abstinence, I can start over and still be loved by support group members. That group acceptance is so tough that we laugh as we share our flaws and imperfections with each other. Just as I've written this last sentence, I've burst into tears because I feel such a need to say that I'm human and that's all that I am. I don't have to be a Supersaint anymore. I love God, and I trust that he can be God. I am his child, only human with many glaring imperfections.

Support groups work because they supply us with so many missing ingredients. We find hope through the love and examples of support group members. We can freely confess our compulsive behavior because we share the same problem and we've pledged to keep information confidential. To judge someone else would be ridiculous. Through our acceptance of one another, we see the unconditional love of God. It disproves the deeply rooted myth that a works-oriented God loves only perfect people.

SPONSORSHIP

This Twelve-Step concept resembles the traditional but nearly obsolete practice of spiritual direction or spiritual friendship, in which two people listen to each other, care for each other, and draw each other out. Direction is usually given more by example than by instruction.

Sponsors are mentors in recovery who challenge you to . . .

- make your recovery important enough that you will report your progress to them regularly
- work on problem areas together
- listen to their experiences and draw hope and strength from them.

A sponsor is someone who has the recovery you want, who has worked the steps, and who uses the tools. A sponsor is abstinent from compulsive overeating and negative thinking. A sponsor should have his or her own sponsor as well.

Your sponsor doesn't become your best friend, although some elements resemble that. You and your sponsor probably won't go shopping together or repair cars together. You spend your time discussing the progress of your recovery, working through difficult issues, and praying for your mutual recovery. If you and your sponsor are buddies, your sponsor may eventually find it difficult to ask you to be accountable for your overeating and negative attitudes.

Sponsors model Jesus' style of authority instead of making a big deal out of everything. For example, before Jesus told the rich young ruler to give away all his possessions, "he looked at him and loved him" (Mark 10:21). He wrapped his challenge up in love. With that in mind, we look for a sponsor who . . .

- does not play God but accepts us when we goof
- is a conduit of God's love, not a usurper of his power
- is a cheerleader, not an executioner.

Your sponsor should be the same gender as you because the closeness that evolves through sharing feelings and intimate thoughts is more than most cross-gender relationships can tolerate. Recovery is a spiritual activity, and when we bond spiritually with a member of the opposite sex, the bonding usually results in sexual activity.

How Do I Choose a Sponsor?

You look for someone who has struggled in a way similar to your own, someone with whom you click. The best place to look is within your support group. Listen to what people say and see whose approach to recovery and abstinence resembles your own. If you don't find a sponsor there, visit other groups.

At the risk of tossing out a cliché, pray about it and tell God that you'll let him lead you to an unlikely or supposedly unqualified person. That's what happened to me. My first sponsor was not a recovering compulsive overeater but a recovering alcoholic and drug addict. For this reason, I resisted asking Jill to be my sponsor for a long time. Jill had walked into our church directly from a drug and alcohol treatment center and asked to join a Bible class. She became part of a class I taught, where her talk about AA piqued my curiosity. Shortly after that I bought my first recovery book, and I began attending an OA meeting that happened to have a companion AA meeting. I told Jill about it and we began riding together. On the way home, Jill was the one who challenged me to start my abstinence once and for all.

In the eating disorders group I attended, I didn't find anyone I wanted to ask to be my sponsor, but I sensed that I needed one. I kept praying and asking God to help me, but I felt he was directing me toward Jill as a sponsor. I explained to God that this was not a good idea (he must have chuckled at my giving him instructions!), but the promptings continued.

In my conversations with Jill, she naturally shepherded me along in my recovery, since by then she had several years of abstinence. One day I finally faced the truth about why I objected to considering Jill as my sponsor. It wasn't that she was a recovering alcoholic; it was that I thought I was better than she. She was the student, and I was her teacher. Who was she to sponsor me?

After that, it became obvious to me that Jill was my sponsor and that she functioned well as one. I asked her questions, and she listened to me and challenged me. I became officially accountable to both Jill and my support group to keep my abstinence. When I knew I was in trouble emotionally, I called her or another recovering friend. I directed my questions about abstinence to fellow recovering compulsive eaters.

This experience taught me a lot about listening to God and following recovery as he prescribes it. I quit being such a by-the-book person and tried to listen to God more.

My experience is unusual, but it shows the importance of surrender. God asked me to look up to someone whom I pridefully regarded as my spiritual underling. It also illustrates the way God may choose an unlikely person to be your sponsor. Are we listening? Are we willing to do something that may not make sense to us?

If you ask someone to be your sponsor and that person agrees, the two of you need to discuss what you will expect from each other.

What Do I Expect from a Sponsor?

Sponsors listen to you share your feelings, but they don't fix you. They don't share what you say with anyone else. If by mistake they reveal what you've said, talk to them about it.

Sponsors share their own experiences, but they do not expect you to follow their path. They allow the Holy Spirit to direct you, and they respect your inner direction. They answer questions, but more often they help you answer them yourself.

Sponsors offer you structure for working the Steps.

They usually read your inventory with you, and they go over your list of those you have harmed and talk with you about how to make amends to them. You may read a book together and talk about it or work through a workbook together. Whatever you do, take more time with issues that trouble you. I've asked those I've sponsored to write an imaginary letter to the person they needed to forgive or someone with whom they were angry. I've asked them to meditate on and personalize Scriptures relating to their myths.

One of my roles as a sponsor is to provide a voice of clarity as people work out their stop-look-and-listen inventories. I try to do this by asking questions in a patterned way so they can eventually do this for themselves:

- How do I *feel?*
- What do I *think?* Is a myth or character defect behind this feeling? What is the truth in this situation?
- What will I *do?* What tools am I going to use to recover the truth? What am I going to do to avoid sabotaging my recovery?

I never assume the role of their therapist or encourage people to sponsor to see me that way. Some of the people I've sponsored have been in therapy, and I respect their therapist-client relationship.

What Should a Sponsor Expect from Me?

When people take the time to sponsor me, they can expect me to follow the guidelines they establish. Sponsors can expect me to call during the times they've said are appropriate, except in an emergency. I will do my best not to intrude in their life, and I will be willing to step aside if I'm not seriously pursuing recovery.

When Does a Sponsoring Relationship End?

We may work with more than one sponsor or change sponsors. Most sponsors have a waiting list, and we need to respect their time. Sponsors should work with people who are willing to work on recovery. If I'm not doing what a sponsor asks, my sponsor needs to challenge me to cooperate or to release me from the relationship. That doesn't mean that we can't be friends; it means that my sponsor will put his or her energy elsewhere. I feel as if I have learned much more from the women I've sponsored than they learned from me. Their calls kept recovery in the front of my mind, and as I would hang up the telephone, I was more surrendered and more eager to have the cleanest possible abstinence.

TELEPHONE CALLS

Calling someone to ask them to listen to you for a few minutes is a bold move. It means you have . . .

- self-esteem: you think you're worthy of someone else's attention
- trust: you risk rejection enough to interrupt someone's life to ask for help
- stopped people pleasing: you called instead of thinking, *If I bother people, they won't like me*
- broken the isolation: you've shared your pain with someone else.

That's why making telephone calls is good for us. We may not have all the above attitudes in place, but we're trying them on when we make those telephone calls.

Mouthing such healthy attitudes can be scary, too, so sometimes I even practice what I'll say before I call someone. Here are the two approaches I use most often:

- "I'm feeling confused by what just happened. Do you have a minute to help me work through it?" (the humble approach).

- "I'm ready to eat everything on the third shelf of my refrigerator. Help!" (the humorous approach).

When we receive such calls, we try to make time for them, and when we do, we usually benefit more than the caller. Many times recovering friends call me because they're self-obsessed or preoccupied with food, and I laugh and say, "Uh-oh. You've named my problem. Start talking!" Together we would work through the problem. Receiving calls helps me.

This tool can be abused, of course. Some people will call seven people to get advice and pit their advice against each other. Usually, this is a subtle attempt to do nothing except talk about the problem.

CONFESSION

The popular recovery saying "We are as sick as our secrets" means that secrecy is what gives our sick behaviors so much power over us. When we release our secrets, we release their power. These secrets include our eating behaviors, our character defects, and even our myths. We confess them to God, to ourselves, and then to others.

Mindy told the support group that even though it was November she still had a stash of candy she bought in a post–Valentine's Day sale. Because the sky didn't fall, and no one condemned her, she closed by making herself accountable to throw the candy away.

As I shared with a recovering friend that I felt jealous of a colleague who was nothing but nice to me, my friend laughed and said, "Those are the hardest ones. They're so nice that you feel even more jealous." I felt a release of the shame of jealousy, and oddly enough, I didn't even feel jealous anymore. It's as if my friend's love for me freed me to love my colleague.

Confession to others not only dissolves the secrecy and shame, it also dissolves the deceit. Deceit is a taskmaster insisting that we become increasingly more deceitful to keep up the facade. Confessing our secrets means the deceit game is over because our recovering friends know our patterns, and we can't make excuses for our binges. We give up deceit, and it, too, loses its power over us.

Confidentiality

The OA tradition of anonymity sets a valuable precedent for keeping confidential what other support group members share. This protects against gossip and ensures that the group will focus on the principles of recovery rather than the personalities in a group.

As churches start support groups, confidentiality becomes even more important, because people in the church see one another in other settings. In such a situation, the temptation seems to be greater to tell secrets outside the meetings.

Confidentiality is rooted in the idea that it's an honor to be the recipient of a confession, and we guard that confession at all costs. No matter how much gossip I hear, I'm not free to reveal what I know about someone in support group. If inaccuracies are glaring, we might suggest the gossiper go directly to the person for correct information.

Accountability

As we confess, those receiving our confession become curious about whether we'll change our behavior in the future. Their curiosity implies a gentle accountability to work at overcoming the behavior.

Sometimes we make ourselves officially accountable to one another to remain abstinent or to carry out certain behaviors, such as giving away any Valentine candy we receive or making amends to a coworker. Part of that commitment is that if we feel we're about to slip, we will use our tools, especially the tool of calling a recovering friend.

Accountability isn't new to us. We've promised ourselves many times that we will stop overeating, but now we're involving other people. We're putting skin on God, so to speak. That means, though, that accountability can be scary. We see ourselves as promise breakers, and if we fail, we have one more reason to beat ourselves up.

The only reason I dared to become accountable for anything was the gentleness I found in my support group and in my sponsor. I knew that I could face them without shame if I failed. Their acceptance kept me from falling into despair and plunging into the addictive cycle again.

Accountability can be a powerful tool. A few months into recovery, I was invited to a party where I knew that a table of treats would be served. I talked it over with my sponsor, and we agreed that I should eat my dinner before I went and eat nothing at the party. "Why don't you take a can of diet soda with you—to help you out if you get hungry?" my sponsor suggested.

A recovering friend told me she was also going to this party and would eat the treats and count it as her third meal. I knew this wouldn't work for me. The party wasn't until 8:00 P.M., and I would eat everything in sight if I waited that long. Besides, the snacks would be laden with sugar, and a meal of sugar leaves me hungover afterward.

So I ate my dinner before the party and tried to avoid the snack table. My friend stood at the snack table for a while, but she was too embarrassed to eat a meal's worth of snacks, so she sneaked out for a hamburger instead.

After she left, I walked over to the snack table and gazed at it. I wanted to have just one piece of fudge so badly. Then I thought about what it would be like to call my sponsor and tell her I'd blown my abstinence. I thought about her valiant recovery from alcohol and drugs and the way my support group members struggled with overeating. I felt a spiritual bond among us all, and I was eager to please them, but in a different way than in my people-pleasing past.

Before recovery my thoughts were, *If I please you, you will like me, and I will feel loved.* In recovery I knew I was unconditionally loved by these people, so losing their love wasn't a factor.

It was as if we were all fighting a battle against the same enemy, and I wanted to do my part. They wanted me to remain abstinent not because I would then become a thin, cool, acceptable person but because it would give me a sane, clear perspective on life. They wanted what was best for me, and we were fighting this tug-of-war together.

As I stared at the fudge, I felt as if my sponsor and my support group were standing there beside me, wanting my recovery more than I wanted it myself. I decided I would wait ten minutes and then come back for the fudge. I walked away. Within a few minutes, I saw someone I hadn't seen in years, and we talked for a long time.

At 10:00 P.M., I remembered the fudge. *Wow,* I thought, *I've almost made it, so I can't give in now.* I went out to the car to get the can of diet, decaffeinated soda I'd brought, and I drank it. I remember sipping on it, licking my lips, and planning how I would share my victory with my support group.

Shedding Those Old Behaviors

I still make myself accountable to my group for my negative attitudes and behaviors as well as abstinence. For a while I made myself accountable to the group to quit yelling at my kids, but that didn't work. So instead, I made myself accountable to use my tools when I felt angry, and that has worked much better.

Being accountable empties our minds of unhealthy choices and puts the healthy one in front of us. We act instead of react. Our boundaries are in place, and we can be ourselves and respond like sane people. Accountability is also a good tool for tying up loose ends. I've worked through many issues and taken a lot of stop-look-and-listen inventories, but some old attitudes hang on. When I worked on a project recently, I felt plagued with thoughts that I was no good at what I was doing, that everyone would laugh at my efforts, and that I had no business working on it.

"Enough," I told my support group that night. "The next time I start beating myself up when I'm working on this project, I'll either stop thinking that way or call one of you."

To my surprise, I stopped thinking negatively. I wasn't repressing the feeling because I've journaled about feeling inadequate and I'm gaining a sense of worth in God's love for me.

What other people think doesn't matter that much to me anymore. It was an just an old, lingering habit.

When I've journaled, prayed, and talked to death certain issues and they hang on like a speck of bubble gum on my shoe, I try becoming accountable for it. Most of the time it works well. When it doesn't and I have to call someone, I don't consider it a failure.

Calling someone has become one more step in the process, and perhaps I did need to talk about it a little more.

If your religious tradition promotes confession in the form of the Sacrament of Reconciliation, make it part of your recovery. If not, promote the art of gentle accountability by becoming accountable to friends, even ones who aren't in recovery, and allowing them to do the same to you. Christians waste too much energy trying to keep each other from finding out what they're really like when they could be helping each other.

SERVICE

As compulsive eaters, we've been so preoccupied with ourselves and our eating that we've become truly self-obsessed creatures. Selfless service moves us outside ourselves, and we think about others' welfare.

Service retrains our thought patterns and takes away our self-obsession. In the past, we spent much of our time thinking about food (Where is that eight-for-a-dollar candy bar sale? Do I have one more brownie mix on the shelf?). We may have served others in a somewhat tainted way, in what Richard Foster calls "self-righteous service," which

- is concerned about impressing others
- requires external rewards
- is concerned about results
- serves friends but not enemies
- is affected by moods and whims
- is temporary instead of a permanent life-style
- is insensitive and can't wait
- fractures community and glorifies individuals[1]

Many of us are involved in self-righteous service and don't realize it. We're serving to boost our self-esteem and feel better about ourselves. Our project is not something that God has laid on our hearts as God spoke to Moses through the burning bush, but it's something we want to do because it will make up for our neediness. This difference can be so subtle that we don't even know we're serving self-righteously until we fail. If failure makes us feel defeated and bitter, we were probably serving self-righteously.

In recovery we turn our thoughts beyond ourselves in true service. This means that I keep my hands off the project because I want God's will more than I want success. If he wants to cancel it at any moment, I can let go. My concern is that I follow God, and success isn't an issue. I can even serve those I dislike to the point that I begin to appreciate them.

Before recovery, I served with mixed motives. I wanted to please God, and I enjoyed many avenues of service, but my service included many elements of self-importance. As a result, I burned out and dropped out of nearly every serving position I held.

When I began recovery, I lived for recovery and didn't serve that much. Every moment of the day I worked to switch my thoughts from food to surrender to God. As time passed, I wanted to be useful to God again, but I didn't want to burn out again. Gradually I tried projects that touched my heart, such as leading a support group.

Many of my friends have followed another pattern. Prior to their recovery, they served little because they lacked confidence and were so preoccupied with food. As soon as they started recovery, they felt so grateful that they wanted to give back. Their recovery gave them confidence and a desire to seek God's purposes in their lives for the first time.

Purpose in Life

Someone recently asked me, "What are we recovering for?" Yes, we're recovering for ourselves. It feels good to shed that obsession with food and feel at peace with ourselves. Yes, we're recovering to be better spouses and parents and friends, and this is exciting. But ultimately these are not enough. We were created by God for his purposes, which can be summed up in the two-part greatest commandment:

- "Love the Lord your God with all your heart and with all your soul and with all your mind."
- "Love your neighbor as yourself" (Matt. 22:37–39).

That means that these recovery tools, both the solo tools and the partnered ones, help me pursue my life purpose, too. It isn't enough to live for ourselves. Here are some words written by Bill Stearns that rocked my heart:

> Think over the energy you're throwing into life now—trying to be the best you can be, trying to get ahead, to be a better Christian, a better family member, a better you. Why work so hard? Why ask so often for God's blessing on your life?
>
> If it's to have a nicer, happier life that's not a bad goal. Especially since that's what heaven will be—an easier, nicer existence. If that were God's purpose for you right now, He would simply take you home to heaven, right? But here-and-now, biblical discipleship is never described as "nice" or "easy."
>
> God wants to bless you. But not to make your life easy. He'll bless you because He's got a demanding job for you—a specific task, one that lays down rails to guide your major life decisions, to keep you from *spinning your wheels in Christian self-improvement.*
>
> Go ahead: Break out of the Christian-culture idea that to join God's family is to become part of a nice, privileged group. It's more like being born into a family business—everybody is naturally expected to take part in the Father's work. Do you know what the Father is doing these days?
>
> . . . What are you doing here [on earth]?[2]

God is blessing us with recovery because he has a purpose for each of us. As we explore our purpose, we get involved here and there and we let God speak to us. God has been challenging me about my purpose in life during those regular times I've set aside to pray and read and meditate. In those moments, I've sensed that I'm to get involved somehow with reaching unreached peoples for Christ, in meeting the needs of the poor in the world, including the homeless around me, and touching them in the name of Christ.

Those are lofty efforts, and I frankly don't know how I could be involved. So far, I've volunteered in projects related to these purposes, and I've written about these efforts. Until I get more direction from God, I'm praying about these causes. My kids laugh at how often we miss freeway exits these days because Mom's head is in the clouds, praying for an unreached tribe in Indonesia or for compassion toward Third World countries in the next economic summit. I'm not saying these things to brag, because I'm doing very little. However, I am finally focused on something besides eating, and it's much more exciting.

You May Be Wondering . . .

Q When I confess to people, am I putting them in the place of God?

A No, as long as you confess to God, too. Confessing to sponsors, support groups, and recovering friends doesn't deny that there is only the one mediator between God and man, Christ (1 Tim. 2:5). When we confess to others, we do so with the knowledge that Christ has performed this mediation. We're taking the next step, expressed in James 5:16: "Therefore, confess your sins to each other and pray for each other so that you may be healed." We appreciate and understand that healing.

Q Do I have to belong to a group in order to become abstinent or recover from my food addiction?

A Some people have been able to work through their issues by themselves or with a therapist, but this is the exception, not the rule. That's because isolating ourselves from others is part of our problem. It not only enables us to hide and eat compulsively but also reinforces our basic mistrust of anything other than food. Partnering with others inserts an objective, "sane" perspective. We not only glean others' insights and sense their mercy but also learn to trust someone outside ourselves (and the refrigerator) for help.

As I've listened to support group friends talk, I've heard in their voices the best parts of myself crying out. I've also heard in their voices what I believe was God's voice warning me, consoling me, and challenging me.

Q Why is it that some people seem to be "hooked" on meetings? Have they switched compulsions?

A My fierce allegiance to attending meetings seems strange to me, since I dislike meetings of other types. When I began my recovery, a support group was the only place I could catch a glimpse of the real me and where I knew that others would see me that way, too. As we move on in recovery, our determination to attend meetings usually corresponds with our determination to gain recovery.

Going to meetings takes on compulsive qualities only when the person becomes self-obsessed and the meetings harm their lives and their relationships. To attend meetings compulsively would mean they would drain the attender's life of energy, while, in fact, meetings usually funnel healthy attitudes into the rest of your life.

PART THREE

How Do I Stay Better?

FOURTEEN

When I'm at Risk

Even though we're changing the handicapped way we used to walk through life, the obstacles we used to stumble over still clutter the path. These can be high-risk moments for us. It's never babyish or weak to brace ourselves and use the tools necessary to walk around these pitfalls. Here are some to consider.

MYTHICAL MOMENTS

David's fears of rejection resurrect themselves during brainstorming sessions at work. He goes to the sessions feeling as if he deserves to be rejected and leaves feeling as if he is the dumbest person in the world!

"Now I go for a long run the night before a brainstorming session," says David. "As I run, I tell God how I fear rejection. I rehearse in my mind all the reasons that rejections aren't personal. I plan funny comebacks. Most important, though, I surrender my need to be wonderful."

If you see a myth appearing on your horizon, prepare yourself. Journal, make a telephone call, or go in a bathroom and cry it out. After a while, your self-talk improves so that you don't need so much lead time to prepare for these moments.

STRESS-FILLED MOMENTS

Sometimes when I reach for the fridge, I pause for a stop-look-and-listen inventory but find there's no traffic in my head—I just want to eat! Then I remember the AA phrase: "H.A.L.T.—don't get too *h*ungry, *a*ngry, *l*onely, or *t*ired." At these risky moments, we look for physical, mental, or emotional refreshment before we put food in our mouths. We shouldn't trust our self-talk in these moments, because it's only self-deprecating. Instead, rest; call a friend; drink a glass of cold water and go for a walk. Then return yourself to life.

I would add another "H": hurry. Cramming too many activities into too little time is a form of perfectionism, and it sets us up for failure. My self-talk is merciless when I'm hurried. On a recent hurried day, it took me a while to be gracious to myself. During my lunch hour, I hurried through errands. I rushed to the bank only to discover that I'd forgotten my purse!

How could I have done that? I raged at myself. *What if a policeman had stopped me? How much would he have bumped up the fine for a ticket because I left my purse at my office? How would I pay for the ticket?*

Easy does it, I told myself. *I haven't been pulled over. I'll go back for my purse.*

So I did. *Uh-oh—that took twenty minutes,* I thought. *A third of my lunch hour is gone.*

So what? I asked myself. *If I don't get every single thing done, I'll do some of it tomorrow. It won't be perfect, but who cares?*

At the bank, I stood in the long line. *Easy does it,* I mumbled and pulled out a book and read.

When it was my turn, the cashier called up someone else instead. *Easy does it,* I mumbled again and prayed that the woman who took "my" spot would have a good day.

As I returned to work, I remembered that I needed to make photocopies of my insurance form. The copy store was next door to the bank, and I'd run off without getting copies.

Even before the negative self-talk could start, I breathed out a huge sigh and drove back to the copy store. In that line, I figured out I would be late for work. *Yes, this means I have to work longer,* I thought, *but this isn't the end of the world. It will all work out.*

Finally, I was done, and on my way back I saw a doughnut shop. The old thought popped up: *I've done so well, don't I deserve a reward?* The new thought replied, *Your reward is that you're not crazy from hurrying. Doesn't that feel good?*

HOLIDAYS

Thanksgiving, Valentine's Day, and even Labor Day can cause us grief because they overflow with feasts and picnics and because we may face relationships that still push our emotional buttons. Here are some helpful ideas.

Plan Your Food

If you can eat the holiday meal at your own home, you can be in control of the menu. You don't have to serve a binge food or fill your table with turkey, dressing, potatoes, gravy, nine side dishes, and three desserts. You might even want to serve the food from the kitchen so it won't be setting on the table only an arm's length away.

If cooking holiday meals threatens your abstinence, avoid it. Perhaps you could go out to eat or eat with relatives. If going to a relative's house is going to provide you with more snacks and feasts than you can bear, stop by after dinner instead. It's not wrong to take care of your abstinence even if it doesn't please others.

Celebrate in Other Ways

In our recovery, we rediscover what true celebration is about—enjoying people, memories, and special traditions. Since food is no longer the center of our holidays, we don't have to spend hours in the kitchen, snacking as we cook.

In abstinence, we're free to focus on people and celebrating. Without the sugar highs, picnic preparations aren't so frantic. Without so much baking and meal preparation, there's time for spontaneous Christmas carol singing around the piano. Without having to ruminate over whether we have everything we need to prepare an elaborate meal, Christmas Eve service is more meaningful.

Adjust Your Expectations

If you had delightful holidays as a child (and we tend to remember them as better than they were), it's tempting to be disappointed if each holiday isn't perfect. If your holidays were marred with squabbling relatives or drunken parents, you may wish you could skip them.

My own problem has been to idealize holidays and expect nonstop Kodak moments. If my kids argue as we decorate the Christmas tree, I find myself grumbling, "What happened to peace on earth?" I'm finally learning to act as if each holiday is any other day and realize that children get so excited that they're bound to misbehave. Since I've given up on our being the perfect family, we're all having a lot more fun.

Keep holidays simple. If Christmas cards don't get sent, don't worry about it. If you're too busy to make Aunt Minnie's potato salad for the Memorial Day picnic, no one will starve.

Dysfunctional Relationships

The sharing at preholiday support group meetings is filled with fearfulness of family get-togethers. We wonder if we will cast aside the games we may have played with family members: I'll get even—I'll be two hours late; I have to bring the most popular dish on the table so everyone will compliment me; I'll tell a long tale of woe about my operation to get everyone's attention and pity.

Although we may still hear others' harsh words or subtle put-downs, we now have tools that we can use. We're building boundaries that act as a shield around us so we can stop incoming data and examine it instead of reacting to it. We can choose to listen to those harsh words, decide if they're useful, and choose the most healthy way to respond.

Once again, it helps to plan ahead. Lena decided not to attend her family's Thanksgiving dinner because she knew that if she faced her uncle who had molested her, she would lash out at him. Marco, whose parents are alcoholics, knew his family would drink at their Fourth of July picnic. He wanted to go, but he didn't want to get upset, so he took a recovering friend with him, and they talked while the others drank.

Therapist Charlene Underhill suggests to her clients that they use their family time on holidays to reconstruct their family tree.

"Everyone loves to talk about themselves, so take an incomplete family tree and ask for help. This gives you interesting genealogical information and also helps you spot patterns of alcoholism, cancer, or suicide. It can get people talking and avoid some unpleasantness."[1]

RELATIONSHIPS

As a compulsive overeater, you probably have many friends and family members who love to eat. We choose friends for our common interests, and eating may have been one of them. This presents us with several dilemmas.

Coping with Those Who May Be Compulsive Overeaters

This is difficult territory because you have to stay away from two extremes:

1. Joining them in overeating. You have to choose between pleasing the people you love and protecting your abstinence. I've served fruit for dessert and watched the faces of my friends fall as they refused to eat it. I was new in my abstinence, and I knew that if I had prepared a gooey dessert, I would have finished it off after they left. My abstinence was more important than pleasing their desire for dessert. Now I could probably prepare that dessert and then send it home with them, but at that point in my life I couldn't do that. I would have eaten as much of it as I could, no matter what.
2. Taking someone else's inventory. Now that we're in touch with our own overeating and our own dysfunctionality, we think we see it in others. We hear the new jargon of recovery and misapply it to innocent situations in life, telling others, "Your diet is so rigid—you must have an eating disorder." In reality, the person may want to lose a few pounds before his college reunion.

Many of us compulsive eaters are vintage rescuers, and we need to back off. We think we can see into people's minds, but we can't. We can't truly understand the processes that go on inside another person.

It's so easy to misjudge others' drives that we should stick to diagnosing ourselves.

Besides, it isn't good for our recovery for us to make judgments of other people. Who are we to insist that someone else has an emotional dependency? We have taken responsibility for ourselves and ourselves only—not the world. That grandiose myth that we could fix the world fueled our overeating for many of us, but we have since discarded it.

If we're truly concerned about friends' overeating, we won't judge or confront them anyway. If they're compulsive overeaters, they need to walk through their own desperation as we have. We can't walk it for them. All we can do is tell our story and leave them with their freedom intact.

Coping with Those with Whom We Still Feel Anxious

Since we used to compulsively eat to manage stress, we find ourselves in a slippery place around those with whom we feel anxious. While we consider the root of the problem by exploring myths and making amends, we need to be practical and prepare ourselves for these times.

We may even need to rehearse responses to keep our boundaries intact. For example, Stephanie decided that she would no longer stumble around apologizing and resenting her boss when he yelled at her. Instead, she would calmly say, "If there's an error, I'll be happy to change it," and leave it at that.

When Stephanie later decided to change jobs because her boss was so harsh, I was surprised. In my own life, I always tried to love the most unlovable people I could find. I neglected my own needs for friendship, and because of this, I had little support in my martyrdom. I thought this was the Christian thing to do.

But Stephanie showed me what the recovery saying "Go where the love is" means. She respected herself enough that she didn't have to live with her boss's verbal abuse. Her example helped me begin to surround myself with healthy people who loved and accepted me. I began to respect myself enough that I didn't have to become a martyr trying to save and serve someone who treats me inappropriately.

What if it's our family members with whom we feel anxious? We don't sever ties with them, but we don't let ourselves be run over, either. We set limits. We don't have to participate in every family activity, and we can say how long it's convenient for them to visit. We set a tone of healthy interaction instead of pity parties, gossip, and overeating.

Coping with Those Who Find Us Threatening

Our friends realize that we are gradually becoming different people. Our new confidence and conviction may threaten friends, family, and especially a spouse. They may not be used to the "new me," who expresses feelings instead of stuffing them. They may not appreciate that we no longer live to go to "all you can eat" restaurants. We may even find that we have little in common with old friends if we aren't eating out or talking about diets or food.

Perhaps you've let your spouse run the show, and now you want to have some say. Perhaps your weight has made your spouse feel justified in being an alcoholic or being overweight, and your recovery has removed that excuse. Perhaps you're no longer overly dependent, and your spouse is afraid your independence will cause power shifts. If you and your friend complained to each other and felt sorry for each other, you are removing the basis of the relationships when you quit complaining. It feels odd to both of you. If your mother enjoyed your dependence on her, she will not be happy that you are asserting your independence.

If explaining your recovery doesn't work, you might ask those who feel threatened to attend your support group with you. Spouses often find it necessary to talk to a counselor together.

If you don't address the issue, these people may sabotage your recovery. I've watched many people stop coming to meetings at the urging of parents and spouses who belittled their efforts. These friends and relatives probably don't mean you harm, but they're acting out of their own neediness. It's as if you and the other person have danced a certain dance step for years, and now you've changed dance steps. These close ones have something to lose by your gaining recovery, and that something is you—at least the old you, who indulged in food and in your character defects. I've been told in different ways by different people that I'm no fun anymore because I don't overeat, gossip, or feel sorry for myself. I'm having more fun in different ways, and I trust that they'll eventually notice that.

TRANSITIONS

It was an early Tuesday morning, and I could feel the craziness taking off inside me. Our home was for sale, and it didn't look like it would sell for enough to help us move to a neighborhood with better schools. A gloom-and-doom predictor was talking about how housing prices were going to crash soon. That night someone would present an offer on our house. What would we do if the offer wasn't high enough? If we accepted the offer, however, I was even more afraid. I felt doubt and even anger that I had to move and leave a home I'd grown to love.

In a few minutes, I had to be dressed impeccably to meet a potential client in Beverly Hills, no less. And the clincher to all this? I'd lost my voice.

I lost my voice, I'm losing my home, I thought. The chaos swirled inside me as I gazed out our sixteen-foot-wide picture window at the peaceful lawn we had cared for. In the next room were two large bags of candy my kids had to take to a party that night. I'd bought a type of candy I didn't like, but perhaps it would taste good anyway.

Sufficient unto the day is the evil thereof, I thought. That old-fashioned wording from my childhood Sunday school days (Matt. 6:34, KJV) came floating back.

So I can't worry about the predicted economic depression. I can't worry about moving. I can't worry about the offer on the house. I can't obsess on that candy.

"Sufficient unto the day is the *chaos* thereof," I spat out my paraphrase. I dug my hands deeper into the pockets of my robe and laughed, paraphrasing again: "Sufficient unto the *morning* is the *chaos* thereof."

I remembered how I'd told on myself at support group the night before, "I'm a control freak, and I'm maxed out." I relived the moment with my friends and released the frustration once more. With that relief and my paraphrased verse tucked between my ears, I dressed for Beverly Hills. One day at a time, one moment at a time.

Even though I was in my fourth year of recovery, the transitions I faced made even candy I disliked seem appealing.

A helpful rule of thumb is to take a year to stabilize our recovery before we marry, change jobs, or move to a different location. That's because recovery already requires so many changes. We discover that we've been walking bent over for years, so standing tall in recovery makes us dizzy for a while. We need that year to begin to discover who we are, so that we choose the new spouse, job, or location using what we've learned in recovery.

RESPECTING RECOVERY'S SPIRAL PATTERN

Recovery isn't so much a line from A to B as an upward spiral in which we learn the same lessons over and over. With each curve of the spiral we recognize our myths and use our tools more quickly.

The spiral gets wobbly when we allow our recovery to get off balance. Our goal is to move through recovery leaning intent on this sturdy tripod of issues:

1. physical recovery: abstaining from compulsive overeating, practicing good principles of nutrition and exercise, becoming comfortable with our body image, looking at physical problems such as low blood sugar that have resulted from overeating, actively serving others in healthy ways to break our self-obsession

2. psychological recovery: writing an inventory, listening to inner drives, healing past hurts, making amends, discovering our myths and answering them with truth

3. spiritual recovery: strengthening our contact with God, evaluating our view of God and correcting it, expressing love for God as he leads us to do

When these issues get out of balance, recovery becomes shaky and may even topple because of the following extremes.

Self-Analysis Gone Wild

"Sometimes analyzing and arranging are sources of relief from hurt," says psychiatrist Dr. Edward Khantzian, "but sometimes they compound it."[2]

Recovery is a time of self-examination, but many of us go overboard on self-analysis: Did I really . . . ? When did I first feel . . . ? Why do I . . . ? We live in our heads as if our whole world stops and starts there. We stand in front of the self-help section of the bookstore for hours. We replace our preoccupation with food with a preoccupation with self and self-improvement.

Recovery is not a lifelong psychological interior decorating project. Our goal is not to become self-obsessed armchair psychologists but to find wholeness and health so we can fulfill God's purposes in our lives. Our overanalyzing is one more manifestation of our self-obsession, and it must go.

Thinking the Pounds Away

It may sound logical that if we discover what's causing us pain and we work through it, our compulsive eating will go away, but it doesn't work that way.

Compulsive eating is a habitual activity that our bodies have gotten used to. We can't eliminate that craving by thinking it through. That isn't enough. We need to practice abstinence, too. Besides, it's abstinence that helps us discover our inner drives. When we're high on sugar, we can't recognize our true feelings.

Feelings That Rule

Without the numbing effect of food, it's easy to live in our feelings. We can splatter our negative feelings across the faces of family and friends with no thought of our responsibility to change. That's why recovery emphasizes writing an inventory and working through character defects.

Spiritual Imbalance

Some underestimate the spiritual nature of recovery, but compulsive eating means that our identity is wrapped up in food. It's not enough to examine our inner issues; we need to reassess who it is that loves us, how much he values us, and his purpose in our lives. Others hyperspiritualize recovery and act as if all problems are solved through prayer. On the contrary: God's will is sought and worked out through our mind, will, emotions, and bodies, using all kinds of tools.

One of the best ways to spot our loss of balance is by attending support group meetings. We may hear someone else's imbalance easily, which prepares us to hear our own. These imbalances flourish when we isolate ourselves, and they simmer down when we partner with others.

You May Be Wondering . . .

Q What can I do about holidays or birthday celebrations that involve late dinners?

A Some holidays, especially New Year's Eve, call for unavoidably late dinners. They're a problem because we get so hungry that we eat much more food much faster than we should. The first time this happened to me, I called a recovering friend, and we agreed on what my abstinence should be that night. I ate a small portion of a very safe food (one I would never binge on) at the normal dinner time, and I ate half of the late dinner meal.

FIFTEEN

Compulsion Hopping

If you take candy from a baby, you'd better replace it with a toy or security blanket of equal or greater value, or you'll hear a lot of screaming.

We often react in a similar way. Abstaining from compulsive eating leaves a void. If we don't consider our inner drives and our distorted view of God, we will fill that void with an equal or greater compulsion or preoccupation.

Many times these new compulsions are behaviors we've toyed with, but now we depend on them to become coping mechanisms. Some compulsive overeaters become abstinent but then spend compulsively, running their credit cards to the limit. Others quit binging, but they yell at coworkers, family, neighbors, and the guy who sells them the morning newspaper.

This occurs partly because things get worse before they get better. Facing our myths is not fun, so we try to deceive ourselves by using another compulsion to cope. "I felt as if I were playing five-card stud," Roger says. "When I became a Christian, I gave up alcohol and drugs and got dealt back overeating. Then I worked on that, and now I'm smoking like crazy. I've got to end this compulsiveness once and for all."

It's not uncommon for alcoholics who are recovering to start overeating compulsively. One recovering alcoholic admitted, "I know overeating is an addiction, too, but at least I won't get arrested for it." Even though our culture says that switching from alcoholism to compulsive overeating isn't so bad, it's actually like changing chairs on the *Titanic*. You're still sinking.

THE MERRY-GO-ROUND OF COMPULSIONS

As compulsive people, we are prone to become obsessed or perhaps what a friend of mine calls "a little bit obsessed." Without becoming rigid or legalistic, we need to look at seemingly benign activities or behaviors before they take over. If we don't, they can distract us from our goal of recovery and keep the drivenness alive in us.

If you're abstinent, expect at least one other compulsion to beckon to you and be ready to tackle it. Here are some of the compulsions and preoccupations to which the overeaters I've talked with have switched.

Caffeine Addiction

Compulsive eaters often switch from eating habitually to drinking coffee and diet cola habitually to keep the stomach full. When I first began recovery, I was told I could drink "all the noncaloric drinks I wanted" between meals. So I did.

Several things bothered me. The first was that the caffeine and sweetener in the coffee and diet cola created havoc with my blood sugar. I could get such a "buzz" off them that I felt crazy. Another was that I could feel the same drivenness developing for caffeine that I'd felt for food, so I imposed a limit on how much caffeine I drank. This forced me to understand that abstinence also involves learning to live on a less-than-full stomach.

Compulsive Spending

Typical compulsive spenders shop till they drop and then some, spending rent and grocery money on nonessentials. Other compulsive spenders put all their energy into making money so they'll have enough money to buy things they don't need to impress people they don't like. Still another variation are the pack rats who feel that possessions protect them from problems. Each little safety pin is a treasure.

This compulsion may begin by occasionally using shopping to alter the mood and feel better. Then they become preoccupied with spending money (or making it or storing possessions) until they develop rituals in their behaviors and feel guilty about them.

We think of shopaholics as a rather cute breed of compulsives. In some circles, it's even trendy for people to brag about how much they shop or complain about having to pay off their credit cards. The issues are still the same, however. Compulsive spenders are using the thrill of acquiring and owning possessions to fill the void in their life.

As Paula became abstinent, she saw the other addiction in her life. "I never drank because my father was an alcoholic, and I saw how destructive it was. As a preteen, I began overeating, and then at fourteen, I turned to spending. Shopping made me 'high.' I talked my mother into buying me a lot of clothes, and I stole them when she wouldn't.

"As an adult, I decorated my house with furniture and trinkets that made me feel good, and I bought new appliances before the old ones wore out. Sometimes I bought things I didn't want and couldn't even use. I was always using my checking account overdraft service and borrowing against my credit card. A few days after a shopping binge, the glow would fade, and I would need a quick shopping trip to sustain me. Unconsciously, I think I even chose my husband because I knew he would be an easygoing, hard worker who would financially support my habit."

Workaholism and Compulsive Volunteering

Some of us become hooked on productivity, and we stay busy no matter what. We're not motivated by a love of hard work; we need to be needed, to control, or to feel productive so we'll feel worthwhile. It's often a reaction to dysfunctional family characteristics: "My mother was an alcoholic, and our house was always a mess," says Elaine. "So I overdid it, mopping my kitchen floor several times a day. It made me feel good about myself."

Workaholics, compulsive volunteers, and busyness junkies work more than is good for them and their relationships. Vivian, a skilled organizer and leader, fetched for her children, served as president of the PTA, and cooked for fund-raiser breakfasts. "It made me feel good about myself and soothed the hurts of my loveless marriage and my rebellious teenage son," admitted Vivian in recovery. "I led the choir even though I knew it would take me away from my family. In fact, I did it to escape my family. Sometimes I was cranky and said insensitive things to choir members, but I thought people should put up with me since I was sacrificing so much.

"The pastor told me I was overdoing it, so I said I would quit doing something, but I didn't," continues Vivian. "Now that I'm in recovery, I see that I was escaping my family. I think I was also angry at the church because they wouldn't let me function in the leadership position I was capable of. I couldn't say that to anyone because I thought women should never express frustration, so I ventilated it through my frantic volunteering."

Bulimic Tendencies

To a recovering compulsive eater and dieter, bulimia looks like the way to have your cake and get rid of it, too. As I listened to bulimic friends talk in my support group about throwing up, overexercising, and taking laxatives, I thought, *Is this the answer?*

Thankfully, I also listened to their pain and saw that bulimia complicates life further. My friend Andrea says, "I still didn't feel good even after I threw up. I felt sick, bloated, and guilty. Yet I kept doing it because I worried about getting fat and losing control. That was part of it—I was a perfectionist. Even though I was thin, I saw myself as huge. I picked at my skin all the time, trying to improve my face. I jumped from one fad diet to another. The recovery program seemed too hard and too slow for me, but I wanted peace in my life. I hated myself. I wanted to live—really live."

While some bulimics have died, many others suffer from severe tooth decay and sore throats. Binging and purging cause disturbances in blood sugar levels and sometimes even cardiac arrest or a torn esophagus. Abusing laxatives and diuretics can cause indigestion and urinary infections and even damage the colon. Repeated vomiting can cause the eyes to become bloodshot, the face to become puffy, the glands to swell, or possibly even the stomach to rupture.[1] Bulimia doesn't even deliver satisfaction for the time being; about 75 percent of bulimics become depressed.[2] As I read about these damaging effects of bulimia and saw them in these friends, I saw that it was not an answer. It was one more addiction I would have to avoid.

Relationship Addiction

"Someday my prince will come," predicted Snow White, and it's also the heart cry of those enslaved to having a partner of the opposite sex. Without a partner, they feel incomplete and can barely function, so they settle for almost anyone. Or they may run from one relationship to another, rebounding into unhealthy relationships, if necessary. The desperation is often so great that there are a lot of affairs and promiscuity to prove to themselves that they're important. The thought is, I need someone, and anyone will do.

Once in a relationship, they cling to their partner so tightly that they suffocate him or her. For many years I expected my husband to fulfill the role of God in my life. He was supposed to magically know what I was thinking or feeling and then say something wonderful that would solve it. I would be upset, and sometimes I didn't even know why, but I expected him to know why and solve it. This left him confused and feeling inadequate because he couldn't perform this way for me. It left me feeling deserted and in despair that he had "failed" me.

In recovery, I saw that I hadn't loved my husband as much as I'd simply needed him. Now I see him as a separate person with deep hurts of his own, and I am his privileged partner, lover, and friend. I cannot fix or control him, be God for him. I cannot save him from his struggles, and he cannot save me from mine.

Media Preoccupation

Nina, a "recovering soap opera watcher," admits, "Those stories were my emotional focus. I daydreamed about the characters, and I cared about them and understood them while I found my own family boring. I almost had a traffic accident one day trying to get home in time to watch one. I would quit watching them, and then I'd see an episode at a friend's house or in a department store, and I'd get hooked again. Finally, after two years of not watching them, I left a friend's house when she turned them on. It's been a lot easier since then."

It wasn't enough for Craig to borrow a book from the library or from a friend; he had to own it, and preferably in hardcover. He wanted to know it would be on his bookshelf if he should want to read it again. Yet one day he looked at his bookshelf and marveled at all the good books sitting there that he'd never read, much less reread.

When does escaping into a string of television programs, sports shows, movies on video, or romance novels become a compulsion? When the answer is yes to the questions below, especially those listed under "distorted attention."

Tolerance: Are you watching or reading much more than what you previously thought was appropriate?

Withdrawal symptoms: Do you get headaches, become nauseous, or become just plain unbearable when you don't get to use this media as you'd planned?

Self-deception: Do you make excuses about why you have to watch or read? Can you admit that you're doing it too much?

Loss of willpower: Do you promise yourself you'll quit overdoing it, but you don't?

Distorted attention: Are you unable to focus on your work or remember details because your mind is obsessed with your television program or romance novel? Does it keep you from getting a job or taking care of yourself or dependent family members?

Many people are afflicted with media preoccupation to a certain extent. For those of us in recovery, this becomes a problem because we don't focus on our recovery as we should. We're too busy escaping—and usually eating at the same time.

Addiction to Rage

We do, and do, and do, and then feel an uncontrollable anger for having to do so much. Especially as we become abstinent, we seem vulnerable to what I've heard called the "dry drunk" attitude. This occurs when former alcoholics find that they're not screaming in a drunken rage anymore—they're just screaming. We can do the same thing. We aren't eating to stuff our feelings, so we get mad. We become hooked on the adrenaline rush that flows when we're in a rage, and it becomes a habitual "high." Like our compulsive eating, we identify it, surrender it, work through it, and become accountable for it.

BEFORE THEY TAKE OVER

The above list is not exhaustive, since nearly anything can be used to numb pain rather than face it. Since preventing a problem is easier than curing one, it's wise to watch out for behaviors or substances that could become addictive in our lives.

Use the questions below based on Dr. Gerald May's characteristics of an addiction to determine if a behavior or substance is a potential candidate as an addiction in your life.

Tolerance

- Are you practicing this habit more and more?
- Does it take more of it to satisfy you?
- Do you no longer feel so guilty about how often you do this?

Withdrawal Symptoms

- Do you miss this habit when you don't practice it?
- Have you tried to stop, and it makes you sad or even miserable?

Self-Deception

- Do you think it's not a problem, although others who are healthy would say that it is?
- Do you blame others that you "have" to do this?

- Do you continue this behavior even though you suspect it is harmful to your physical or psychological self?
- Do you hide the extent of your involvement with this behavior from spouse and friends because they won't understand?

Loss of Willpower

- Have you promised yourself you'll stop, but you haven't?

Distortion of Attention

- Do you plan parts of your days around this activity, looking forward to it?
- Does focusing on this make you forget about most everything else?
- Do you change plans—perhaps even purposely isolate yourself—to indulge in this behavior?
- Do you find that you "need" it to feel better?

Talking It Out

Our neediness can be subtle and difficult to separate from healthy desires. We may wonder if we're volunteering because God is leading us to do so or because we want to feel productive and admired. That's where talking in a support group or with recovering friends helps. When I was offered a book project a few years ago, I couldn't decide if I should accept it. It was in my field and looked like a great idea, but I know I fight being hooked on productivity. As I explained the opportunity to a wise recovering friend, she said, "You don't really want to do it, do you?"

Startled, I asked her why she said that.

"Because you keep trying to convince me that it's a good idea. I don't think you're convinced that it's a good idea for *you.*" She was right. As I searched my heart, I realized that I didn't want to do it, and

I turned it down. I consider that a milestone in learning to keep myself from becoming a workaholic.

OVERCOMING OUR NEEDINESS

How can we keep from switching compulsions and overcome our neediness? The first line of defense is to face our myths as we become abstinent. Simply "white knuckling" it through abstinence is a diet. "When you arrest one addiction, you move on to another unless you deal with the core issues," says Dr. Patrick Carnes. "In the addiction community, we need to do a better job of dealing with the core issues and not be so focused on the specific addictive behavior."[3]

Another line of defense is to decide once and for all that no external substance or activity can solve our problems and make us feel good again. "Our throw-away culture looks for external solutions to internal problems," says Dr. Carnes. "We don't like to deal with limitation, with death, with spiritual issues or issues of meaning in our culture. The result is that we're an addiction-prone culture. People pick solutions that get them through instead of ones that make them whole."

Still another line of defense is to surrender the drive to feel good. Our culture tells us to do whatever is necessary to find happiness. Even the United States Constitution talks about the right to "life, liberty, and the pursuit of happiness."

Advertisers tell us that it's important to feel good, and we believe them. At times, the church borrows this thinking: love and serve others because it makes you feel good inside. A "successful" worship service or Bible study is one that makes us feel good.

This drive to feel good corners us into using a compulsive behavior. I don't feel good, so . . .

- I'll starve myself because then I'll look good, which makes me feel good.
- I'll work longer hours, even if takes me away from my family, because it makes me feel good.

- I'll spend money so I can dress well and drive a fast car and feel good about myself.

As we discover and correct our myths, we face this ultimate question: What takes first priority: a healthy, recovering life (which, for me, includes spiritual growth) or temporary good feelings?

The answer sounds obvious, but that doesn't mean it's a simple one. Once we make the decision to surrender this drive, the issue is at least settled. It reappears many times, and over and over again we have to surrender that drive to feel good.

You May Be Wondering . . .

Q Couldn't those characteristics (tolerance, withdrawal symptoms, self-deception, and the like) be true about the way people feel love to their spouse and show it?

A Yes, but the difference is that a marriage is based on interdependence, not a one-sided dependency. A healthy marriage is usually free of that unhealthy drivenness of being so "hooked on" the spouse that your physical and spiritual well-being suffers without that person. There's no self-deception or loss of willpower because there's nothing wrong with being devoted to your spouse.

Q Isn't there such a thing as a positive addiction? Aren't there people such as Mother Teresa who adopt a single-minded purpose for their lives and pursue it?

A This is not an addiction because Mother Teresa does not neglect her own hygiene, diet, or rest. Those who work with her volunteer to do so, and they are not manipulated or controlled by her. Her life is not out of balance; she doesn't neglect her health or a family to do her work.

Jesus lived this balanced life. When pressed, he backed off and went to the desert for solitude and rest and renewal (Mark 1:35, 6:31). God's will is for us to find what we want to do and go for it but to maintain a balanced life-style.

Psychologist Dr. Peter Robbins once mentioned in an interview, "It's a curious thing about addictions. There's a thin line between love and anger, between genius and madness, between the addictive person and the creative, productive person. Turning a high-energy person into a couch potato isn't helpful. As a therapist, I must help a person maintain vigor for life but channel it so that it's productive and not undermining. Accountability to a therapist or group setting is necessary."

SIXTEEN

Do My Kids Have to Be Compulsive Eaters, Too?

Every time my kids used to ask if they could buy a candy bar, or when they snitched curls of cheese from the food processor, something inside me pinged. *Oh, no,* I worried, *are my kids going to be compulsive eaters, too? Are they becoming emotionally dependent on food?*

At other times, I've worried about my worry. Will my kids react to my overconcern by starving themselves? I recognized my paranoia several years ago, and I've toned it down. But . . . did I catch it quickly enough? Will my kids eat normally?

When I've felt beaten by my compulsive eating and ready to trash my recovery, one hope has kept me going. I don't want my children to have to fight this same battle with compulsive eating—or to react to my struggle by becoming bulimic or anorexic. This desire has acted like a steel rod propping up my spine and making me get up and fight for my own recovery.

THE PATTERN CONTINUES

Randy Rolfe, therapist, mother, and author of *Adult Children Raising Children,* told me a story that resembles many others I've heard in support groups:

> Lucinda [not her real name] didn't have an outward eating disorder, but she had a preoccupation with eating. She was afraid her daughter would inherit her own mother's obesity. She

> watched the daughter's eating so closely that the daughter thought eating was everything in life. To signal her independence, the daughter stopped eating. So there were the obese grandmother; Lucinda, the mother who somehow succeeded in being picture perfect; and an anorexic granddaughter.
>
> The first thing I wanted Lucinda to do was come to terms with her mother's obesity. Lucinda couldn't be herself around her daughter because she feared that she or her daughter would become obese like the grandmother. Lucinda has to accept that she is a different person from her mother and forgive her mother for imperfections. Then she won't have that fear. Parents fear most for their children what they hate about themselves or what they hated most as children in their parents.[1]

If we don't work through our negative feelings toward ourselves or toward overweight parents, we overreact to these feelings. We create myths such as "our whole family is doomed to be overweight" or "being overweight is the worst thing that can happen."

Facing our self-loathing helps us dethrone food and being overweight as our worst enemy. We make peace with food and with our body shape. This becomes one more piece in the puzzle of recovery.

PASSING ON NEEDINESS

We worry that we've not only modeled compulsive eating for our children but also behaved so dysfunctionally that we've created pain and neediness in our children. We're afraid that neediness will drive them to eat compulsively. Here are some common tendencies I've heard parents who are compulsive eaters talk about.

Controlling

We're tempted to control not only our children's actions but also their thoughts and feelings. We may even impose our views and choices on our children.

Barbara McFarland says that she often sees parents trying to control their children's eating: "Let's say a youngster makes a food choice that is not the best—two or three helpings of potatoes. Do you feel that a child shouldn't have two helpings? Why not? They may not make wise choices all the time, but who does? No one does, especially kids who are three or four or five."[2]

Some parents exert control over children by demanding respect. They don't allow children to ask questions or voice opinions because it threatens their authority. They may go so far as to act as if children don't deserve respect. This isn't specifically said but is implied through actions and tone of voice.

Know-It-All Parents

Parents who know the Bible well may especially feel that they have special insight into what is right and wrong in every situation. This is also subtle, but it shows itself by the way that teenagers often complain: "I wish my parents would admit when they're wrong," or, "I wish they didn't think they were right all the time," or, "I wish they would listen to me when I talk."

Frozen Parents

Parents who were physically or sexually abused as children often shut down their feelings at the time of the abuse. As parents, they fear making the same mistakes, so they may not discipline children or show affection. Said one parent, "I'm afraid of how much power I have over my children. What if I misuse it? I was abused. What if I abuse my children?" She thinks that if she can't do it right, she won't do anything at all.

Parents Looking for Parents

When parents look to their children for comfort and fulfillment, the roles reverse. Children take on heavy emotional and perhaps even physical burdens of adults so that they grow up needing comfort and fulfillment as well.

Hypervigilant Parents

When we're hypervigilant, we act and react out of fear. If our family of origin was chaotic and argumentative, we may eliminate normal childhood arguments by forbidding them: "Just be quiet. I heard arguing throughout my childhood. I can't stand it now."

Some hypervigilant parents are so afraid their children will be exposed to harsh people or abuse situations that they refuse to let their children have normal childhood freedoms. Their kids can't play with neighborhood kids unless their parents are watching them; their kids can't spend the night with any of their friends.

Suspicious Parents

Denise tells how she used to come storming into the kitchen if she heard the sound of her children opening the refrigerator door. "One time my son was munching out on leftover cake, and I grabbed it out of his hands and threw it in the trash can. Now I'm trying not to panic but to see these times as opportunities to teach my kids when and how to snack and just how much is too much. Also, I accept that some sneaking around is normal in all children."

Our fear and suspicion send messages that food is forbidden, even magical, and so we promote overeating when we're trying to avoid it. While we do want our children to feel healthy guilt for wrongdoing and to choose not to repeat it, our overreactions communicate shame instead of healthy guilt. This can create an inner neediness in children that too often they relieve with more munching.

John Bradshaw explains the difference so well: "Guilt says, 'I've done something wrong'; shame says, 'I am a mistake.' Guilt says, 'What I did wasn't good'; shame says, 'I am no good.'"[3] As we deal with our own shame, we recognize our own shaming tone of voice or the way we roll our eyes at our children's mistakes.

PASSING ON RECOVERY

Since I modeled my compulsive eating for my children for several years and I still battle it, it's safe to assume that my children are somewhat affected. I've asked myself what has helped me most in recovery, and I try to supply some of that for my children. Here are those things I need and how I see parents providing them for their children.

Parents Acting as "Sponsors" (or Models)

The best thing parents in recovery can do for their children is to work on their own recovery. This supplies their children with the best version of their God-given parents, coping and rebuilding their life. Here are some specific attitudes and behaviors we can model as if we were "sponsors" to our kids.

Viewing Food and Weight "You have to be a role model about your body image, your weight, and your preoccupation with food," says Barbara McFarland. "I would suggest that you monitor the messages you give your child about body, weight, and food, especially around mealtime. Write these messages on a note pad for two weeks. Include nonverbal messages too such as facial expressions of disapproval; they can be worse than verbal ones."[4]

Toni didn't realize what messages she was sending her daughter until her daughter said, "Mom, you have fat legs!"

"Then I realized that she was only repeating what she'd heard me say many times," said Toni. "So I explained that my legs aren't really fat and that sometimes I worry because I want to look like the women in the fashion magazines. I finally explained to her that most women never will look that way and that they shouldn't worry about it."

We often mix our messages about food, too. We eat a cookie and look at our kids and say, "Cookies are bad for you." When they say that Mom has fat legs, we're hurt, but they are only repeating what they heard us say. Monitoring the messages we give our kids helps us because then we're more careful about what we say to ourselves, too.

We often have to admit and accept that we may never have that perfect pencil-thin shape that our culture says is so important. As we make peace with food and with our body shape, we have less to fear for our children.

Modeling Healthy Outlets "If you fear that your child is eating as an emotional outlet," says therapist Randy Rolfe, "you need to model other ways of working through emotions. You might say, 'I feel overworked. I think I'll take a walk. Do you want to walk with me?' or, 'I'm bored. Let's do something together. Do you want to read *National Geographic?*'"

Passing on Healthy Self-Talk The self-talk that has helped you will probably help your kids, too. As a recovering perfectionist, I recognize perfectionism in my daughter, and I can whisper to her as I mutter to myself, "Progress, not perfection." Just as I have to correct the shaming way I talk to myself, saying to myself, "I did cause that problem, and I don't have to feel guilty about it," I sometimes have to correct the way I talk to my kids. I back up and make amends: "I was wrong to say that you're always late. Sometimes you're late, and sometimes you're on time." More and more, I'm adding, "But no matter what you do, I'll always love you." This is no doubt a version of my self-talk that reminds me that God loves me no matter what.

Respecting Their Boundaries A sponsor or friend helps us by not trampling our boundaries, and we do the same for our children. Our attitudes and words, such as the following, communicate appropriate boundaries.

- "I won't discount your feelings." In the past I've brushed aside my children's feelings because I was in charge or because I thought they didn't fully understand the importance of what I was doing. It's taken me a while to learn to search for compromises and consider their wishes. I've tried to learn to treat my children as courteously as I would treat another adult.
- "I give up control over you." Respect means that I surrender that drivenness to control my children. I offer consequences, but I don't coerce or manipulate them. I don't forbid them to have certain friends, but I point out attitudes: "Do you see how this friend is bossing you around? How do you feel

about that? What could you say to her when she does that?" I leave the rest to them.

- "I won't limit you because of me." I let them eat potato chips (even sour cream and onion!), but I leave the room. Barbara McFarland says, "You have to keep the boundaries clear. I'm the one with a problem with food. *This kid is going to have a problem with food only if I make it a problem.*"[5]
- "I let you make your own mistakes." A recovering friend had worried that her eight-year-old daughter was overeating and had talked to her about it. She worked hard at not saying too much, however. Finally, at a Thanksgiving dinner after she had told her daughter she could have two desserts, the daughter sneaked four instead. The daughter threw it all up in front of the dessert table, which embarrassed her and made her realize that stuffing herself was not fun after all. Says Mom, "I'm glad I didn't take it too hard because I see now that this needed to happen. She rarely overeats now."
- "I give you permission to control your own spiritual life." We can teach our children spiritual tools, and we can share our experiences, but their spiritual lives are between God and them. At the age of twelve, Jesus surprised his parents by having his own spiritual direction of which his parents weren't aware. When Jesus stood in the temple in Jerusalem that day and said, "Why are you searching for me? Didn't you know I had to be in my Father's house?" part of what he was saying was, "Even at my age, I have to pursue my spiritual path in my own way" (Luke 2:49).

Growing in Our Confident Attitudes We let our children see that we're struggling with a difficult job, but we keep trying. We laugh at our own mistakes, which shows that we've stopped taking ourselves so seriously. As they watch us stand up for ourselves appropriately, they're more likely to have the courage to yell or get away if someone attempts to molest them. We model for them our newfound ability to approach problems with creativity—to consider the choices, to create new alternatives. We show them that we do control what is within our ability to control, and we leave the rest to God.

Parents Acting as a Support Group

We can help our children the same way that support groups help us in the following ways.

Expressing Feelings Even though we express feelings well in support groups, we may still hide anger and sadness from our kids. "If kids see parents suppressing their emotions, they will do it, too," says therapist Randy Rolfe. "Parents need to be able to say, 'I've had it today. Bear with me.' Caring parents are sometimes afraid to do that because they don't want to overburden their kids."

Beyond expressing our emotions, we need to create a safe atmosphere in which our kids can say what they're feeling. We can also help them acknowledge, identify, accept, and express those feelings, just as we're learning to do.

Randy Rolfe says this is important because articulation is a large part of knowing what you're feeling. Even children with expressive faces whose feelings are easy to read need to be able to say what they're feeling.[6] We can give them access to feeling words with this simple question we ask ourselves: "Do you feel mad, sad, glad, or bad?"

Others need even more direction. I found a chart with names of feelings and appropriate faces above them for my less articulate child. When she tells me her feelings by pointing to the "frustration" face, with its drooping eyes and squiggled mouth, her own face relaxes. We both feel better because she has communicated her anxiety to me.

If your children are adolescents or older, you might invite them to talk about their resentment toward you: "I wasn't the perfect parent. When you were little, I should have . . . . Let's talk about it." This not only disentangles the relationship, it also shows them that people can admit failures and go on.

Admitting Struggles When our children tell us they feel lonely because they've changed schools or embarrassed when they wet their pants during a giggle fit, we listen to their hearts. We take off our policeman's uniform or cheerleading outfit and listen for feelings of embarrassment or hurt. We may even tell them about times we felt hurt or left out, and we don't always have to give our stories pretty endings. We tell what happened, how we felt, and perhaps how we might do things differently now.

As we work on our character defects, we can tell them about our progress. When it's appropriate, we can ask their forgiveness and make amends, which becomes a model for them.

Learning to Lighten Up Even if we've damaged our children's self-esteem (and what parent hasn't?), we can build it by telling them what they're doing right. We don't withhold affection even when they misbehave. We can be fun and show our silliest side of ourselves to our kids often. All this reinforcement is free of charge—they get it whether they get perfect scores or failing grades.

"Perfectionism feeds into eating disorders," says Randy Rolfe. "If you see eating disorder tendencies in your child and you're sure you haven't projected perfectionism, you should check other influences. Is the other parent perfectionistic? Does the child feel inferior to a brother or sister? I have yet to find an anorexic daughter without a perfectionistic parent. There's a lack of acceptance of who she is."

Parents Acting as Information Givers

Parents aren't controllers, notes John Bradshaw, but simply reference librarians.[7] Just as we receive information in recovery books and from friends, we dispense information to our children about life and how it works, especially in the following areas.

About Compulsive Eating At appropriate times, we explain what it means to be a compulsive eater and perhaps even about abstinence and the process of recovery. Since children of overeaters are prone to constant dieting, bulimia, or anorexia, we need to explain the destructiveness of these disorders, too.

About What's "Normal" If you grew up in a dysfunctional family, you may not know what wise and "normal" parenting is like. We don't need to feel embarrassed to take parenting classes. Many helpful ones are offered by therapists, churches, and adult education departments of local school districts. They talk about child development and what's normal for children at certain ages. When we understand children's natural stages, we aren't so quick to label their newest streak of independence as a sign that we're ruining them!

Networking with well-adjusted parents helps, too. We beat ourselves up when it seems like only our children squabble for hours on end. (Often a perceptive friend or relative points this out to us in lofty tones.) Then we talk to other honest parents and hear that their kids have been bucking the system and each other all week, too. Then we realize that this is normal behavior!

THE GOOD ENOUGH PARENT

Some of us have repeated the same perfectionistic, destructive pattern in our parenting we used in weight control: striving for perfection, overcontrolling, failing, and feeling guilty and hopeless. This pattern is listed in the left column in the following table. Look at how these tendencies show themselves in weight control (middle column) and parenting (right column).

Pattern	*Weight Control*	*Parenting*
strive for perfection:	perfect diet	perfect kids
overcontrol:	rigid dieting	strict parenting
failure:	quit the diet	we and our kids fall short of perfection
feel guilty, hopeless:	"I'll always be overweight."	"I'll never be a good parent."

These tendencies don't work with weight control; they don't work with parenting. The more I work at being a great parent, the harder I am on myself and my kids. I've overdosed on so many self-help parenting books and classes that I feel defeated as a parent, which translates into even poorer parenting.

So I'm surrendering my need to be a great parent. I work my recovery, do the best I can, and enjoy my children. This attitude is expressed well in the following "Twelve Steps of Recovery, Revised for Parents."[8]

1. We admitted we were powerless over our ability to protect our children from pain and became willing to surrender to our love and not our control.
2. We found hope in the belief that recovery is possible through faith and a willingness to work on ourselves.
3. We reached out for help and acknowledged that we are not alone.
4. We took stock in ourselves as parents.
5. We learned to share our parenting issues with others without self-recrimination.
6. We became ready to change by giving up the demand to be perfect.
7. We made conscious changes in our parenting by identifying specific strategies for healthy parenting.
8. We took responsibility for the effect our parenting has had on our children and learned self-forgiveness.
9. We made amends to our children through healthy parenting without overcompensating.
10. We modeled being honest with ourselves and our children and created acceptance in our families for imperfection.
11. We learned to accept our limits in life and found our true spiritual paths while allowing our children theirs.
12. We reached out to other parents in the spirit of giving and community.

You May Be Wondering . . .

Q At what point do I put my child on a diet?

A When you ask this question, consider first that parents, especially those who struggle with food and eating, often mistake natural childhood growth spurts as weight-gaining trends. "We can't predict growth spurts, so we get nervous when our children develop differently from others," says Randy Rolfe,[9] also a trainer in health issues.

Rolfe cautions that allergies can make children seem to eat compulsively. "If they won't let go of food with milk, corn, wheat, or eggs in them, they could be allergic to one of them. That means that this food stimulates their bodies and creates a craving for those foods. You may want to read more about this because it's difficult to diagnose, but allergies can make a dramatic difference in their eating and their behavior."

If the child is indeed overweight, therapists familiar with eating disorders caution parents that the first issue is to look at the model they're providing and begin to work on themselves. "Look at the family system—why is overeating a coping mechanism for the child?" says therapist Charlene Underhill.[10] "If you're working on food issues, you can model and even discuss ways to express feelings and cope with troubling emotions. You share this as one person with another, not as a controlling parent."

Second, look at the child's diet. "Most children who are overweight eat foods that are high in fat, sugar, and salt, such as chips and soda," says Randy Rolfe. "Sometimes parents defend their children's diet by telling me their kids eat a lot of hamburgers, which are high in protein. They forget that too many hamburgers provide too much fat."

Taking a child, especially a boy, to a diet group, can be punitive and shameful, says Underhill. Whatever we do with weight control, we don't want to plant in a child the guilt and shame of the addictive cycle. Many diets create that shame if you "blow it," or kids feel shame because they've disappointed their parents.

"Rather than putting children on a diet," says Rolfe, "it's more important to get on their side. Then we can educate them about hidden fats and sugar in food as we show them how to avoid using food as an emotional outlet."

"Getting on my children's side" can be an important peripheral benefit of examining my own attitudes toward food. I can allow God to renew my mind and to show me how to deal with myself and my children in more reasonable ways.

SEVENTEEN

Challenges of a Growing Recovery

If you look at the cover of any tabloid at the supermarket, at least one headline will refer to sex and another to weight control. Our culture has shaded these two issues in such a way that abstinent compulsive eaters may struggle with them even if they've been in recovery for years.

When we look in the mirror, we don't see our true images. Instead, years of mythical thinking have distorted our attitudes toward our body, and we see an overweight, asexual image of ourselves. Recovery involves facing our feelings and thoughts about our body image and our sexuality. Then we redirect our thinking until it falls into healthy, realistic patterns.

NEVER THIN ENOUGH

When we say that we're recovering compulsive overeaters, our culture says that means that we used to be obese and now we're pencil thin. That's not always true, because some compulsive overeaters managed to stay within twenty pounds of their average weight through frantic dieting, and, for various reasons, many abstaining compulsive eaters never become thin.

The latter frustrates many of us, especially on anniversaries. "Look," we say, "I've been abstinent for a few years, and I'm still not as thin as I'd like to be."

If you've experienced this type of frustration, consider the following questions. (In this discussion I am forced to use the "C word," "calories," a topic with which we compulsive dieters easily become obsessed. But this discussion isn't about calories or diets; it's about knowing the way our bodies work so we don't get frustrated with ourselves.)

1. Is my abstinence sensible?

   It's possible to have an abstinence of three large meals a day and simply feel thankful that we're no longer eating between meals. This isn't a wise long-term abstinence because we're still giving in to the drivenness of food, even if it's only three times a day. This also violates the rigorous honesty we have adopted, because we're not eating three moderate meals, we're binging three times a day.

   Even if you're sticking with a sensible abstinence, it's easy to get discouraged. A sensible abstinence is usually a normal way of eating, and it doesn't promote immediate weight loss the way a diet does. It takes a while for our body to use up the excess pounds and return to our average weight. Sometimes those last ten to twenty pounds seem impossible to lose.

2. Am I following sound nutritional standards?

   Am I eating more food than my body needs? Rigorous honesty demands that we determine if we're eating the proper amount of food to sustain our goal weight (roughly sixteen to twenty calories per pound). We may be abstinent from overeating, but we can still be dependent on (or compulsively eating) sugary or high-fat food. Eating these kinds of food contribute to being overweight and drain us of our energy.

   One nutritional reality that we often forget is that the older we get, the less food we need to eat to maintain the same weight. For example, when a woman passes menopause, her energy requirement is about 15 percent less than it was when she was in her twenties, yet her nutritional requirements are basically the same.[1] So the older we get, the more "nutrient-dense" our food needs to be in order to maintain our goal weight. There's less room for "empty" food with low food value and high calories.

Am I giving my body the exercise it needs to stay healthy? Since our bodies were meant to be active, we gain weight if we eat normally and never exercise. We don't need to center our lives around exercise or even view exercise as a weight loss technique. We exercise simply to feel fit and have energy.

3. Do I have a healthy concept of normal body weight?

   Most people in contemporary culture, especially women and even more especially compulsive dieters, have a distorted body image. To us, being normal means being thin.

   Almost 77 percent of all women think they are overweight, while only 25 percent are, says Charles Murkofsky, director of the Eating Disorders Program at Gracie Square Hospital, New York City. " 'In order to obtain the kind of thinness that is currently in style, many women need to go to extraordinary lengths to control their diets. The belief that our basic worth as human beings is measured by how thin we are is extremely dangerous and, regrettably, quite prevalent,' Murkofsky says."[2]

   This distorted view of female body image in our culture has been chronicled (and somewhat dictated) by media standards. A study by the City University of New York showed that Americans in the media, especially females, are much thinner than their counterparts of twenty years ago.[3] The ads for diet foods and body-slimming products are significantly higher in women's magazines than in men's magazines. The result is that in recent times women feel pressured to be thin.

   Because of this cultural pressure, it is a rare woman who doesn't allow the media to distort her body image and who doesn't measure her self-worth by how thin she is. She understands that she doesn't have to be thin to be attractive or to be hired for certain jobs or to feel good about herself.

4. Have I chosen the best goal weight for my body?

   If you have a healthy concept of normal body weight, you won't choose your goal weight based on the hope that you will look as sleek as Cher or Tom Cruise. The physical focus of recovery is to eat normal and healthy meals and to maintain a healthy body, not to be able to model swimwear.

Dr. Judith Stern, professor of nutrition at the University of California, Davis, says that people who have lost weight but still don't have a perfect shape may have unrealistic expectations. "Look at the people who model swimwear—they're underweight and young. Most people will not be underweight, especially if they start from being overweight. And when you're thirty, you're not going to look like you're eighteen."[4]

Holding an unrealistic hope for thinness harms us because it increases the self-loathing we're trying to shed. Reaching for an underweight look can discourage us to the point that we're ready to hop on the addictive treadmill once again with compulsive dieting, bulimia, or even anorexia.

How do you choose a realistic goal weight? Stay abstinent and find a nearly average weight at which your body functions well. Some choose a goal weight that is too low because they haven't considered that the biological influences, such as those listed below, may be working against their efforts.

Genetics

Eating and exercise are not the only players in the game of losing weight. Our genes also influence body weight and shape, which feels unfair because we have no control over this issue.

Recent studies show that the genetic influence is strong. Dietitian Janis Jibrin writes, "A University of Pennsylvania study of 3580 adult adoptees in 1986 found that their body weight was closely linked to the weight of their biological parents and not at all to that of their adoptive parents."[5] She goes on to say that if a child's parents are not overweight, the child has a less than 20 percent chance of becoming overweight, according to recent studies. If the child has one overweight parent, the odds increase to 40 percent. If both parents are overweight, there's an 80 percent chance of being overweight.[6] It seems that those of us with overweight parents fight not only physical, psychological, and spiritual battles but also a biological tendency.

No one knows for sure how genes affect us, but it looks as if our genes influence our body shape and the amount of fat we burn and store. For example, Dr. Stern says that genes influence the resting metabolic rate and how many calories we burn during exercise.[7] This means that even though my friend and I eat and exercise in identical ways, one of us may burn more calories because of a different genetic makeup.

Yo-Yo Dieting

The cards are also stacked against those of us who dieted so much that our weight went up and down like a yo-yo. Repeated weight loss and gain further slow a person's metabolism, which means that we need fewer and fewer calories to maintain a normal weight.[8] Dr. Stern tells about the results of a study in which patients used the same weight loss program for a second time. Either they took longer to lose the same amount of weight or they didn't lose as much weight in the same amount of time.[9] This means that those of us who spent years yo-yo dieting can expect our excess weight to come off at a discouragingly slow pace.

Below-the-Waist Fat

Hips and thighs seem to be the last thing to slim down, which also frustrates us. Body shape is also under genetic control, which is why C. Wayne Callaway, M.D., associate clinical professor of medicine at George Washington University in Washington, D.C., goes so far as to say, " 'It's futile, frustrating and self-defeating for a woman to try to get rid of her hips. Women practically starve themselves; they wind up feeling sick, dizzy, cold and depressed and too thin everywhere but their hips.' "[10]

If your eating habits are abstinent and nutritionally sound and you have chosen an average goal weight but not reached it, you may feel understandably frustrated. You may have arrived at a weight that is comfortable for your body but not for your mental image of a perfect you.

Consider the risks in hurrying the weight loss and nursing your discontent with not being thin enough:

- You'll have to go on a very low-calorie diet, which could propel you into the cycle of compulsive dieting, bulimia, or anorexia.
- If and when you achieve a thin figure, you may pay a price for maintaining it. That price is a lifelong preoccupation with food and weight control. Recovery frees us from our fixation with calorie counting and having to be constantly on alert about food and weight gain. Do you want to go back to that? Will it enhance your recovery? Will it promote joy and peace in your life?

STAYING OUT OF THE CORNERS

We can work our recovery better if we don't corner ourselves into being thin. Recovery involves becoming content with an average shape and weight, even if it is not as thin as our culture deems attractive. Wishing for a perfect body is "part of the magical thinking that is demythologized in recovery," says Dr. Barbara McFarland. "There are all different body shapes and sizes. You face the reality of what your body is. It's that old problem of accepting reality. You say, 'This is the body I have. No amount of weight loss will change this.' Once you accept the truth of who you are and what your body is like, you have been set free."[11]

Beating ourselves up for not being thin works against our recovery. "As we focus on our physical being and whipping it into shape," continues McFarland, "we're expending energy that detracts from our ability to focus more on our spiritual being. This body deteriorates and dies. If you believe in life after this, then you need to spend more time and energy on that."

Dr. McFarland also notes that focusing on thinness sabotages us from living in the present. "As long as you were busy worrying about your body size and wishing you were a size three, it was a distraction from being present in your own life," says McFarland. "It keeps up that old fretful business that distracts you from what really matters about life. Once you accept your body size, you wonder, *What do I do with myself now?*" Abandoning our obsession with thinness becomes one more piece of the recovery puzzle.

RECLAIMING SEXUALITY

In almost any support group of compulsive overeaters, the second-most-talked-about subject (after food) is sex. Either we love it or we hate it, and it's often the latter. One of the challenges—and joys—of recovery is making peace with our sexuality.

Dodging Our Sexuality

Barbara McFarland and Tyeis Baker-Baumann have noted in their book *Feeding the Empty Heart:*

> Compulsive eaters are often fearful of sex and of their sexual feelings. For the overweight compulsive eater, her weight shields her from these feelings and protects her from physical intimacy. An average weight compulsive eater may be sexually active, but her only desire may be to please her partner, hoping her partner will take care of her sexual needs. This often doesn't happen, leaving the compulsive eater feeling inadequate and worthless.[12]

We may have chosen to boycott our sexuality because we didn't understand it, we didn't like it, or it scared us. Being sexual creatures made that difficult, so we used food to help us.

Eating: the Problem Solver Eating compulsively not only shielded us from our sexuality but also seemed to solve so many sexual problems, such as these:

- The threat of extramarital sex: My extra weight keeps those I'm attracted to from noticing me.
- My fear of sexual involvement: When having sex scares me or my sexual appetite scares me, I can eat and feel better.

One woman said that her late night snacks were more satisfying than having sex and that the extra ten pounds kept her husband away.

- My unfulfilled sexual desires: Eating provides sensual rewards when an uninterested spouse snubs me. If I have a sandwich before I go to bed, I will be satisfied and ready to sleep and won't need to think about sex.

In recovery, we find that dodging our sexuality hasn't solved our problems at all. It added to our self-loathing and harmed our marital relationship. We cut off part of who we are, and that left us limping.

Unlearned Skills It makes a lot of sense that we compulsive eaters have not nurtured our own sexuality or a healthy sexual relationship. They call for skills we've just begun to work on in recovery, such as these:

- Letting ourselves go: We have been extremely self-conscious, especially about our bodies.
- Communicating sexual needs, likes, and dislikes: We have numbed our needs and feelings with food, so we're not used to paying attention to them. We want so desperately to be loved that we have appeased our spouse and forgotten our own needs.
- Trusting our partner: We haven't trusted any person for years; we've trusted only food.
- Risking: We want to control our environment and the people around us.
- Working at mutual enjoyment through trial and error: We view every error as a courtroom trial in which we are condemned or we condemn others. We don't do anything unless we're sure we can do it well.
- Enjoying ourselves without controlling the situation: We have felt threatened by intimacy and found that uncontrolled pleasure feels wrong.

The large percentage of compulsive eaters who were sexually abused as children have complicated layers of feelings about sexuality that must be dealt with. How can I betray myself by enjoying sex? It takes courage and often professional help to work through these issues.

Reclaiming our sexuality is one more level in the upward spiral of our recovery. We need to come to terms with trust, risk, communication, and pleasure on yet another level. As usual, we use our tools. Excellent literature is available to read, especially *Sexuality and Compulsive Eating* by Barbara McFarland and Tyeis Baker-Baumann (see Appendix 3). Meditating on the Song of Solomon shows us that God plans for us to trust, risk, and find pleasure. We talk through our fears and goals in a journal or with a sponsor, therapist, or support group and finally with our spouse if we are married.

Awakened to Sexuality

As Alice became abstinent, she found herself thinking constantly about a movie star who always played sexual hero parts. "It may sound silly, but I made myself accountable to my support group to stop watching movies with that actor in them. If I didn't do this, I found myself fantasizing about him. I tried to tell myself that it was OK to daydream about him as long as the fantasy didn't include a sexual encounter. But too often it did. It made me feel dissatisfied with my husband, so it had to go. I'm so grateful that my support group understood."

Why did this happen to Alice? Overeating and sexuality often have an either-or relationship, so that when we stop overeating, our sexual drive returns. We're no longer stuffing our feelings or going to bed on a full stomach. Suddenly, we're awake and interested in sex. Recovery helps awaken our sexuality also because we're removing the mistaken identities we may have placed on our spouses. Many recovering women I know have realized that they used their husbands to fill the void in their childhood father-daughter relationship. We wanted a man who would wipe our tears and cuddle us, and we tried to squeeze our husbands into that role of our father. At some level, our conscience kicked in and said, This is a father-daughter relationship—you're not supposed to have sex with him! So we tried to avoid it.

In recovery, we're reparenting and comforting ourselves in healthy ways, so we've quit treating our spouses like parents. Now we see them for who they are, and we feel free again to enjoy a sexual relationship with them. We're surprised, and so are they.

Problem solved? If abstinence or weight loss awakens your sexuality, try to explain this to your spouse. It's as if you're starting over. You're rediscovering the sexual side of your partner and appreciating his or her strengths and weaknesses.

Don't expect it to solve all your problems, though. Often, your spouse is so confused he or she will not respond the way you expected. Your spouse spent years living with the barriers you put up and now must adjust. If your marriage has been troubled, don't assume that it will automatically improve because your sexual appetite has returned. Even if it isn't troubled, this change may affect your relationship so much that you need marital counseling to come to terms with it and other changes in yourself. That isn't bad; it's an adjustment to a healthy way of life.

As we meet each challenge in recovery, we're not alone. We have a sponsor and a support group. They offer us the opposite of the tabloid newspaper: They understand instead of exploit; they accept instead of sensationalize.

You May Be Wondering . . .

Q When I have reached my goal weight, do I have to remain abstinent?

A There may be some recovering compulsive eaters who do not remain abstinent after reaching their goal weight, but I haven't met them. The rule of thumb is that abstinence never ceases. Every time I've thought I didn't need to be abstinent any longer, I looked food in the eye and found that it was still too alluring.

When psychiatrist Gerald May discusses addictions (and he considers eating disorders addictions), he says that the "brain never forgets what it has learned." He explains, "Since multiple functional systems are involved [in the brain's learning to be addicted], the learning becomes entrenched."[13]

Our brains remember how to "do" our compulsion as easily as we know how to ride a bike even if we haven't ridden in years. For this reason, Dr. May sees the wisdom in addicted persons considering themselves "recovering" rather than "recovered."[14]

Q What are some beginning steps in reclaiming my sexuality?

A Some people dodge their sexuality with poor grooming and sloppy clothing, so these are prime areas to examine. You might reconsider behaviors or clothing normally associated with your gender that you have shunned. Is that because you honestly don't like them or because you don't feel adequate enough to try them out? I've heard recovering men talk about weight lifting for the first time—one guy bought a pair of cowboy boots he'd always wanted! This goes along with the advice therapist Charlene Underhill gives her female clients about buying pretty lingerie no matter what size they are to help them affirm and appreciate their sexuality.[15]

Underhill also suggests to married women who have been victims of sexual abuse that they reclaim their sexuality by initiating sexual intimacy themselves, especially in nonsexual ways such as massage. "This helps many victims feel more in control rather than wondering when the advances will come. It's important to remember that they are having a sexual relationship with someone *they've* chosen; they are not victims."

EIGHTEEN

New Freedoms in Recovery

Growing in recovery is like wearing a special coat that's been hanging in your closet with your name on it. The day you find out it's in there, you open the door of the closet, peek in, and shut the door quickly. You're confused, terrified, and even a little elated by this new approach to life. After a few weeks of peeking every day, you open the closet door and stare at the coat, trying to understand it. One fine day, you put it on for an instant, shudder, and then hang it back up. You do this for months until you notice that you leave the coat on a little longer each time. After a while you're wearing the coat daily and loving it.

You feel confusion, terror, and elation in recovery because you look at life differently, and you wonder just how comfortable you should be "wearing" your recovery all day. Occasionally, you reach out for the old myths, but you're ruined for those old attitudes. The new ones are growing on you, and you can't go back.

NEW VIEWS OF OURSELVES

Ideally, we have been learning these new attitudes throughout recovery. If not, they attack us once we've lost some weight, and they may terrify us. If we don't wrestle with them now, we put ourselves at great risk of letting them overpower us so that we lose our abstinence. Here are some of those new healthy attitudes.

I Can Be Attractive

Perhaps we lived in sweat pants and baggy clothes, and now it's scary to wear short sleeves! It's foreign to think about picking out clothes that flatter us and that might attract attention. We question whether we deserve to look attractive or deserve to have fun trying.

I Can Be Comfortable with My Body

"Body image is a concoction of the imagination," says Barbara McFarland. "Since most women have a distorted body image, you want to work on building a friendly relationship with your body and the image of it, instead of an adversarial one."[1]

We can experiment with being comfortable with our bodies by trying different kinds of massage or exercise or body movement. I see now that this is what I was doing when shortly into my recovery I began to feel free to dance without worrying about getting the steps right. I'd always been too self-conscious to let go in front of others, but in recovery I just did it. When my husband and I attended his office party and his coworker told my husband that he thought I was a great dancer, I was surprised.

I couldn't believe that I had changed so much.

I Am Sexual

People of the opposite sex may begin looking at us for the first time, and we may not feel comfortable with that. It doesn't mean we've lured them or that they will necessarily hurt us. It just means that we're normal, sexual people as God created us to be. Our boundaries are intact, and we know how to respond without overreacting.

I Can Be Competent

You may have hidden behind being overweight as a way of letting people know that they shouldn't expect much from you. That way, you pleasantly surprised others by your competency. Now they see you as an average person, and they're not dazzled by your average competency anymore. You have to work harder to dazzle them, and perhaps you've stopped being so concerned with dazzling them at all.

I Can Eat in Front of Others

Maybe you used to think that everyone was watching to see how much you ate, and you felt embarrassed eating with other people. I used to worry about what I ordered at a restaurant if I was sitting with thin people.

Once while eating with a group of recovering people, I felt self-conscious and figured I should order a salad. *Wait a minute,* I told myself, *you can order a steak if you want it.* It felt odd to stop worrying about what other people thought. It felt even more odd that when I gave myself permission to do this, I realized I wanted the salad more than the steak.

I Can Feel Normal About Food

Before recovery, food was either our best friend or our worst enemy. Recovery helps us eventually make peace with food. This means that food quits haunting us. We can make a poor choice of food and not beat ourselves up over it. We decide to choose more wisely next time.

Even with the foods that still drive me, I know it's a process of making myself accountable to someone to choose how much, if any, I'll have of them. Food is no longer a security blanket or a bogeyman. It is a source of nourishment, simply F-O-O-D.

I Feel Empowered Instead of Weak and Useless

As we shed our myths and feel more comfortable with ourselves, it's normal to feel elated and even overactive. We're free to be who we are, but who we are scares us. What will we do with this newfound freedom? Will we now dress provocatively? Will we defy people who have been authority figures in our lives? If we do, will they retaliate?

We eventually come to terms with this new empowerment by using our tools. We call our sponsor, journal our deepest feelings, talk at support groups, and listen to ourselves. We funnel this new empowerment into our service opportunities, creative activities, and companionship with God.

I Can Trust Myself Again

In recovery it gets easier to make decisions because there's less traffic in our heads. We're not so clouded with myths. When we make decisions, we can keep in mind our myths and character defects and make allowances for them. For example, we hurriers know better than to take a night class this semester because it will cause us too much stress.

Another gift of recovery is trusting our intuition. Our intuition is the part of us that figures things out but we're not sure why or how. Before recovery, our drivenness dominated our intuition, so we didn't trust it. When we sensed something was true, but we weren't sure why, we figured it was our old craziness, so we didn't trust it. In the past when I sensed that I wanted to be good friends with someone, I didn't pursue it because my myths told me that no one would want to be friends with me. As our abstinence and subsequent clarity grow, we sense our intuitive thoughts more clearly. We know things in our "knower" for the first time in years. This is one of the intriguing gifts of recovery.

These new views of ourselves can be scary, but we can afford to be patient with ourselves. Recovery never stops. We remain as patient with ourselves as we were in losing the weight. Surrender means we don't give God a deadline for overcoming our problems.

FREE TO TAKE CARE OF OURSELVES

Now that we've stopped eating so compulsively, we aren't masking our inner voices. We're listening to our needs and trying to figure out how to meet them in healthy ways.

For the first time in my adult life, I go to bed when I'm sick. I've always played the martyr, trudging through snow to go to college classes when I was sick and working with piles of tissues on my desk when I had a cold. Now I even go to the doctor when I need to instead of thinking everything else is more important.

I follow a saying I heard in Twelve-Step groups, "Go where the love is," and I don't do business or form close friendships with people who don't treat me with respect. It's not worth it to partner with people with whom I feel miserable. It makes me want to eat, which I'm not going to do. My old pattern was to form friendships and work relationships with people who criticized or belittled me in some way. I thought that loving my enemies meant I had to count them as best friends, but that isn't so. It simply means that I treat them with kindness and respect.

We avoid getting ourselves into jams. We don't take on positions of service we don't like, but instead we serve in the ways God has gifted us. We speak up to people who talk down to us. We don't feel guilty when we take vacations.

FREE TO ESCAPE IN HEALTHY WAYS

Giving up food as our best friend and worst enemy leaves a practical, as well as emotional, hole in our lives. If I'm not hunting down doughnut shops all the time, what will I do? We use healthy escapes.

Healthy escapes are activities that we genuinely enjoy but never seem to have enough time to do: sports, reading, taking walks, or working in the yard. Using our healthy escapes on a regular basis keeps our inner selves alive. They relax and refresh us so we don't feel so needy when our hurts surface.

Psychotherapist Fran Hill of Torrance, California, teaches classes on healthy escaping and notes:

> From time to time you need to return to a child-like place of playfulness. There you abandon concern about past or future. In this place of living only in the moment, your anxieties diminish. This helps you attain a larger sense of fulfillment and balance so

> you won't get to the end of your rope so easily. For example, you might want to build into your schedule several times a week to sit down, close your eyes, and listen to music for a half hour. For others, it may be getting involved in their favorite sport.[2]

Since Fran Hill often works ten-hour days, she plays tennis three times a week.

> When I get out on that court, I am totally present in what I'm doing. My responsibilities and anxieties disappear. This good feeling offsets the stress of my work. Building it into my schedule is a necessity, not a frill.
>
> You have to think ahead of time about what pleases you and schedule that into your life. Too often people wait until the last minute before realizing they need to break the tension. Then they find themselves unprepared without a healthy escape at hand. So they reach in desperation for quick, easy, and, above all, familiar outlets. Overeating is a common substitute for healthy escaping.

We may even be able to use our healthy escapes to distract ourselves in the height of our obsessive thoughts about food, those days when everything looks like an ice cream cone—the clouds, your jacket rumpled on the chair, even the stack of dried leaves in your yard.

I also use healthy escapes when I feel sad but can't figure out why. I've used my tools—taking a stop-look-and-listen inventory, journaling—but the feelings remain. So I challenge my kids to a game of basketball or I take a bike ride or call a friend to chat or wash the car so I'll feel productive. Not everything is explainable, so I don't even try to understand it.

Can your work be a healthy escape? You can tell the difference between a healthy escape and a compulsive preoccupation, says Fran Hill, by the aftereffects. "Healthy escaping is energizing. You return to your responsibilities more committed, capable, and productive. But compulsive behavior leaves you dissipated." If your work exhausts you, it's not a healthy escape; if it exhilarates you, it probably is healthy.

A healthy escape usually gives balance to your life. Just as a physical activity such as tennis balances Fran Hill's intense mental and emotional involvement with her clients, so solitude can restore active people. Says Judy, a busy office administrator, "When I get overwhelmed by life, I go down to the beach. Working hard makes me feel scattered. Strolling on the beach makes me feel centered."

MAKING THE MOST OF TIME

In my compulsive eating days, I loved activities that made time pass quickly because that meant it would soon be time to eat again—or past time, so I could eat a lot! Now I treasure timelessness for a different reason: It's the time I feel most alive and in touch with God. I have a sense that this is what eternity will be like.

Activities that create a timelessness are ones in which we don't bother to look at the clock for more than an hour. Time and schedules melt away because what we're doing seems true and real and touches the deepest parts of ourselves. We may sometimes use them as healthy escapes, but they are more than that; these are moments in which we experience our true purposes in life.

These timeless activities become more possible in recovery. Our recovery equips us with a love for solitude, honest sharing, and selfless service that make these timeless activities flow better. As our recovery puts us in touch with our true life purposes, we seek out these timeless activities. In recovery, we gives ourselves permission to spend chunks of time on these timeless things we once thought were frivolous. We even make them a priority.

Creative Activities

Recovery relaxes us, which allows us to be more creative in the activities we love. That can be anything from arranging flowers to building furniture, from thinking up a new solution to an old problem to putting together a new outfit with clothes we've had for years.

I could never explain why I thought recovery enhanced creativity until I read the traits describing the "creative personality." The following list of traits of the creative personality was developed by psychologist Abraham Maslow and others.[3]

- high amounts of energy, enthusiasm, and a general zest for living
- a well-developed sense of humor and the ability to laugh at yourself
- a high level of tolerance for uncertainty and ambiguity
- a problem or project orientation (being a problem solver)
- a need for and ability to make productive use of solitude
- independent thinking and a tendency to question conventional wisdom

When I read that list, I sat bug-eyed and laughed. Here's a list of similar attitudes recovery is giving me.

Energy: I have more lasting energy (as opposed to caffeine or sugar energy) and can work through depressing times.

Humor: I've always loved to laugh, but now I that I'm shedding my perfectionism, I can laugh at myself and my imperfections.

Tolerance for uncertainty: I've surrendered my need to understand and manipulate everything. I've accepted that there are many things I'll never understand.

Problem solving: When problems occur, I'm not as likely to waste time blaming someone or feeling sorry for myself. I look for solutions.

Solitude: Journaling and pouring out my soul to God have made me not only love solitude but also schedule it regularly into my life.

Independent thinking: In my recovery, I'm giving up my know-it-all attitude, which is causing me to find answers in unlikely places. Often they are the opposite of what I would have guessed them to be.

Questioning conventional wisdom: There used to be only one right way to do anything. If I didn't already know it, I would figure it out from a library book. Now I see that there are often many good ways to do the same thing.

Look at the creative things you do and enjoy the added creativity that your recovery brings to them.

Concentrating on God

People talk about looking at the minutes slowly tick as they try to put together a five-, ten-, or fifteen-minute "quiet time." Before my recovery I tried to have a quiet time because I knew it was good for me, and the time dragged. My quiet time now follows a regular but unorthodox schedule that I happened upon accidentally. The minutes and sometimes hours fly by too quickly. I sense God's presence, and in these moments, I forget myself completely and walk and talk with God. Now that I can relax and enjoy myself better, I seem to be able to relax and enjoy being with God more, too.

The same is true in church when we're worshipping and singing to God. It's over too quickly. I have more I want to say to God. I don't want to leave our interaction so quickly.

Spending Time with Friends

"Where has the time flown?" I often say to my friends after a Sunday afternoon walk in the park. We talk about issues of great meaning to us—feelings, dreams, progress in recovery—and we share ourselves. We appropriately call them "time outs," and they are. We laugh about the things we once cried over, we look at life through someone else's eyes, and we come away with new energy and new hope.

In recovery, we make time for these timeless moments even if it's inconvenient. Even though I loathe getting up early once a week to meet a friend for breakfast at 6:00 A.M., that's the only time she can meet, so I do it. But by the time we're huddled over the coffee in the quiet restaurant, we're either giggling or sharing our newest secrets. These timeless moments of renewal balance some of the pain of my recovery and the drivenness that still comes back to haunt me.

THE SIMPLIFIED LIFE-STYLE

Trying to do and be everything our culture expects stirs that old drivenness within us. Now that we aren't repairing our faltering self-esteem and trying to please others, we determine what we're good at and what we're not good at, what we like and what we don't like, what we want and what we don't want.

For example, now that I've given up compulsive spending, I've discovered that I hate shopping, so I order from catalogs and I enlist the help of family members who are born shoppers. In my former, more compulsive, days, I became president of every organization I joined and organized it to the hilt because I needed that feeling of importance. Now I can admit that I dislike organizing things, so I decline all the glory of holding executive offices and offer to do what I do best—teach or lead small groups. I'm not anxious to own new gadgets that need service contracts or a big house on the hill that will take a lot of effort to clean. What I have is fine, thank you.

This has quieted my compulsive tendencies. I see that I needed to prove my self-worth with all my frenzied shopping, organizing, and owning. I treat myself better now because I can relax, and, not surprisingly, I'm having more fun.

GIVING BACK

Losing makes you a winner (Matt. 10:39). We see these opposite forces at work in the way that Christ gave up his life on the cross and came back as a "winner," showing us that life is forever and that we can have that life, too.

Giving back gives back. The idea that we receive by giving back works in recovery as we find that sponsoring someone fuels our own recovery. As we use our tools, others ask us about recovery, and we share our experience, strength, and hope as one beggar telling another where to find bread (Step Twelve). We also give back by leading meetings and even starting new meetings.

If you would like to start a new Overeaters Anonymous meeting, you need to send for a starter kit from the World Service Office of Overeaters Anonymous (listed in Appendix 3). There is a small fee for the kit.

You might want to start a support group within your church (see Appendix 2). This is a useful way to introduce recovery to your church since overeating is a compulsion that some find easier to admit than other compulsions. (If you do start a support group, make sure that it is clear that this support group is not an OA meeting. OA is autonomous and not affiliated with any political or religious organization or doctrine.)

Why bother starting a support group in your church as long as Overeaters Anonymous exists? OA groups work well, but sometimes those who already have an established faith in God find that recovery is a process of repairing a breech with God. We come to recovery angry with God, and we have a lot of Judeo-Christian "God stuff" to work through in the group. This can sometimes be difficult for those of other faiths to understand or tolerate. We usually need a sponsor and other recovering friends who appreciate our struggle because they share our personal but omnipotent view of God.

Starting a group in your church also creates the opportunity to worship side by side with people you've been rigorously honest with. At your meeting you share your struggles; in the worship service you sing words that proclaim God as the conqueror. Struggle and worship are a powerful combination, and they build a kinship I've found in few other groups. Confession and praise were meant to stand alongside each other. When they do, we experience genuine fellowship.

ENJOY THE CHANGES

As you move into years of recovery, you see your progress. It used to be that when I made a mistake, a courtroom scene played out in my mind. A pencil-waving prosecutor would accuse me, and a pasty-faced judge would condemn me. I felt like a condemned person who would never overcome anything.

Finally, I sense that the courtroom scene in my mind is fading, and I'm replacing it with a support group scene. People are wearing sweaters, and they're leaning in and resting their elbows on their knees. They're looking at me with gentleness and honesty. I'm telling them that I have done something foolish once again, and they give me accepting, lopsided smiles.

God has quieted the traffic in my head, gathered my broken places together, and taught me to surrender myself. When I fail, it's OK. It's never too late to start over again.

APPENDIX 1

The Twelve Steps and Twelve Traditions of Overeaters Anonymous

THE TWELVE STEPS

Listed below are the Twelve Steps of Overeaters Anonymous, with appropriate Scripture accompanying each one. (The following comparison of OA's Twelve Steps with Bible verses is the author's own interpretation and should in no way imply endorsement by OA. OA is not affiliated with any public or private organization, political movement, ideology, or religious doctrine.[1]

1. We admitted we were powerless over food—that our lives had become unmanageable.

   Scripture: "I know that nothing good lives in me, that is in my sinful nature. For I have the desire to do what is good, but I cannot carry it out" (Rom. 7:18).

2. Came to believe that a Power greater than ourselves could restore us to sanity.

   Scripture: "For it is God who works in you to will and to act according to his good purpose" (Phil. 2:13).

3. Made a decision to turn our will and our lives over to the care of God *as we understood him.*

Scripture: "Therefore, I urge you, brothers, in view of God's mercy, to offer your bodies as living sacrifices, holy and pleasing to God—which is your spiritual worship" (Rom. 12:1).

4. Made a searching and fearless moral inventory of ourselves.

   Scripture: "Let us examine our ways and test them, and let us return to the Lord" (Lam. 3:40).

5. Admitted to God, to ourselves, and to another human being the exact nature of our wrongs.

   Scripture: "Therefore, confess your sins to each other and pray for each other so that you may be healed" (James 5:16a).

6. Were entirely ready to have God remove all these defects of character.

   Scripture: "Humble yourselves before the Lord, and he will lift you up" (James 4:10).

7. Humbly asked him to remove our shortcomings.

   Scripture: "If we confess our sins, he is faithful and just and will forgive us our sins and purify us from all unrighteousness" (1 John 1:9).

8. Made a list of all persons we had harmed and became willing to make amends to them all.

   Scripture: "Do to others as you would have them do to you" (Luke 6:31).

9. Made direct amends to such people wherever possible, except when to do so would injure them or others.

   Scripture: "Therefore, if you are offering your gift at the altar and there remember that your brother has something against you, leave your gift there in front of the altar. First go and be reconciled to your brother; then come and offer your gift" (Matt. 5:23–24).

10. Continued to take personal inventory and when we were wrong promptly admitted it.

    Scripture: "So, if you think you are standing firm, be careful that you don't fall" (1 Cor. 10:12).

11. Sought through prayer and meditation to improve our conscious contact with God *as we understood him,* praying only for knowledge of his will for us and the power to carry that out.

    Scripture: "Let the word of Christ dwell in you richly" (Col. 3:16a).

12. Having had a spiritual awakening as a result of these Steps, we tried to carry this message to compulsive overeaters and to practice these principles in all our affairs.

    Scripture: "Brothers, if someone is caught in a sin, you who are spiritual should restore him gently. But watch yourself, or you also may be tempted" (Gal. 6:1).

CHRISTIANITY AND THE TWELVE STEPS

As Bill Wilson, the founder of Alcoholics Anonymous, was seeking sobriety, he attended meetings of the Oxford Group, which proposed to reclaim "first-century Christianity" (its focus changed later). Bill Wilson borrowed from this group its emphasis on examining self, admitting character defects, making restitution, and working with others.[2] He never adopted the Christian faith, and he wanted Alcoholics Anonymous to be as pluralistic as it now is so it could retain its focus: alcohol recovery.

The Steps remain, however, grounded in Christian principles (except that the nature of "God, as we understood him," comes from the Bible). I believe that because some of these principles have been overlooked by the twentieth-century church, those of us in the Christian faith can and may find not only recovery but also new biblical dimensions to our already established faith in Twelve-Step principles.

THE TWELVE TRADITIONS

Here are the Twelve Traditions that originated with Alcoholics Anonymous and have been adopted by OA and other Twelve-Step groups.[3] They have helped Overeaters Anonymous groups stay focused on recovery and attain a sense of unity, even though OA welcomes people of all faiths and no faith. This unity has eliminated unnecessary distractions, which has contributed to OA's success in recovery from compulsive eating.

1. Our common welfare should come first: personal recovery depends upon OA unity.

2. For our group purpose there is but one ultimate authority—a loving God as he may express himself in our group conscience. Our leaders are but trusted servants; they do not govern.

3. The only requirement for OA membership is a desire to stop eating compulsively.

4. Each group should be autonomous except in matters affecting other groups or OA as a whole.

5. Each group has but one primary purpose—to carry its message to the compulsive overeater who still suffers.

6. An OA group ought never endorse, finance, or lend the OA name to any related facility or outside enterprise, lest problems of money, property, and prestige divert us from our primary purpose.

7. Every OA group ought to be fully self-supporting, declining outside contributions.

8. Overeaters Anonymous should remain forever nonprofessional, but our service centers may employ special workers.

9. OA, as such, ought never be organized, but we may create service boards or committees directly responsible to those they serve.

10. Overeaters Anonymous has no opinion on outside issues; hence the OA name ought never be drawn into public controversy.

11. Our public relations policy is based on attraction rather than promotion; we need always maintain personal anonymity at the level of press, radio, films, television, and other public media of expression.

12. Anonymity is the spiritual foundation of all these Traditions, ever reminding us to place principles before personalities.

HOW OVEREATERS ANONYMOUS BEGAN

In January 1960, three women met in a living room to share their experience, strength, and hope for recovery from compulsive overeating. One of them, Rozanne S., had taken a friend to Gamblers Anonymous a little over a year earlier and been touched by the feeling that she was no longer alone. She could tell that others at the GA meeting felt the same feelings of inadequacy, fear, and self-pity that she felt. Even better, they were able to arrest their compulsion, and she wanted to do the same thing with her compulsive overeating. She searched in vain for a group that addressed overeating the same way but found none.

So Rozanne and two others began their own informal meeting. By the end of 1960, they were interviewed on a syndicated television show and received five hundred letters. The next year they published a directory that listed fifteen meeting places, and in 1962, they held their first national conference. A few years later, a grateful member sent her story and the address of OA to "Dear Abby," who printed them. The group received seven thousand letters. Now thousands of groups around the world meet.[4]

APPENDIX 2

Starting a Support Group in Your Church

If you think God wants you to start a meeting at your church, wait. Listen to see if that is what he is really saying or if you're trying to rescue others or make a name for yourself.

As you're listening to God, talk to others in your church to see if there's any interest. It takes at least five or six interested people to start a support group, so that when some are absent, there are still a few to share. Are enough people interested that you would have at least four each week? You may need a general support group for people with all kinds of compulsions in order to have enough people.

HOW TO BEGIN

In the meantime, continue to attend a support group of some type for compulsive overeaters and work on your own recovery.

Group Leadership

Church-related support groups usually require a permanent leader to keep contact with the church leadership. If you sense a go-ahead from God, look around for a core group of at least two other people who would be willing to help you start this. Our old habits of saving the world alone are gone now, and we know the value of partnering with others. Will they help set up chairs and make up flyers, or will this be your sole responsibility? Some responsibilities within the group may be rotated so that leaders don't burn out.

Church Support

Explain your idea clearly to the pastoral staff and see how they react. Make it clear that support groups involve honesty that is shocking to unwarned church members and that the group may attract non-Christians who don't have the same language or behavior standards as church members—in fact, it should reach out to others and show them that God loves them no matter what. Can they accept this?

Some church leaders find it hard to believe that a bunch of people can sit around and share their stories without an expert present to fix them. You may wish to explain the group's purpose in light of 2 Corinthians 1:4: "We can comfort those in any trouble with the comfort we ourselves have received from God." Support groups are one way that Christians can live out this text. It generally stuns leaders to hear that the Holy Spirit can lead in this way, and as a result, they will need to have a lot of faith in you and your recovery to trust that it will work.

In rare instances, a member will talk about abusing a child or wishes to commit suicide. Since many states legally bind teachers, pastors, and other church representatives to report these instances, the leaders of your support group need to relay these to the pastor and let him or her take the proper steps. Be wise about making a report, however. Talk to the suicidal person afterward to see how strong his or her intentions are. When a woman in a support group I led revealed her detailed plans for a suicide, I told my pastor immediately. He called her husband, who thwarted those plans and persuaded her to go to a counselor.

Group Ground Rules

Talk with your fellow leaders about the ground rules for the group. Confidentiality is especially important in a church because people already know one another and it's easy to tell others who attended the group when that should not be revealed.

Here are some sample group ground rules that you may wish to use:

1. When others are talking, we let them finish without interruption. (This is called the "no crosstalk rule.") We save our questions until the end, and we even let the person who is crying finish their sharing without "rescuing" them.
2. We come to listen, to support, and to be supported by each other in the group, not to give advice. We do not fix each other. Questions are saved until after the group is dismissed.
3. We speak in the "I" form instead of "we," "they," or "you." This helps us take responsibility for our feelings and accept them as being valid. We do not blame others for our behavior.
4. We keep sharing to no more than five minutes in order that others in the group will be able to share.
5. We try to share from the heart as honestly as we can. It's okay to cry, laugh, or be angry in the group without condemnation from others.
6. What is shared and whom you see in the group are to stay in the group and not to be shared with anyone else.

These ground rules roughly follow the principles of the Twelve Traditions of OA, and they are blunt enough that people unfamiliar with support groups can understand them. Support groups vary in their effectiveness, and these ground rules can help a group fulfill its primary purpose: to create a safe atmosphere for sharing.

This atmosphere is violated when members are judgmental or give advice even in supposedly helpful ways. The "no crosstalk rule" eliminates these problems because it prohibits remarks, side conversations, or responses of any kind. This may seem rigid unless you remember that a support group is often the first place that people feel safe speaking about their experiences or their confused feelings about God. A response that you think is noncommittal may easily seem judgmental to others because they're treading in such new, uncharted territory. This tone helps all participants because we are often learning to listen to others without rescuing them or giving advice. Listening well is one more way to quell our grandiosity.

Format

I prefer to stay as close as possible to the general format of Overeaters Anonymous meetings because they have worked so well. Also, if someone visits the group from OA, they will be comfortable because the format is familiar.

Choose a format that works well for you. Here's one that I've used:

1. Leader for that evening introduces himself/herself and welcomes the group.
2. The group repeats the serenity prayer: God, grant me the serenity to accept the things I cannot change, the courage to change the things I can, and the wisdom to know the difference.
3. Volunteers from the group read the Twelve Steps of Overeaters Anonymous and other introductory readings they choose.
4. Newcomers introduce themselves and give a sentence description of why they came. Leader passes the hat and explains that a contribution of fifty cents or a dollar helps parents with child care.
5. Leader reads the guidelines for sharing and invites participants to share on a chosen topic (anger, humility, self-pity, and the like) for no more than five minutes. Leader may impose time limits in order for everyone to share. Leader may open or close the sharing.
6. Meeting adjourns promptly, and sufficient time is allowed for talking afterward.

You might choose to begin by reading through these Tools for Recovery together.

TOOLS FOR RECOVERY

Literature

We read brochures, daily meditations, and books on recovery from compulsive overeating.

Prayer

We involve ourselves in gut-level honest prayer, revealing our darkest secrets and deepest feelings to God. We invite God into our recovery process and learn to relate to him as the parent we've always been looking for.

Scripture

We no longer beat ourselves over the head with verses, but we use the Scripture to relate to God in a healthy way, to pour out our souls before him. Paraphrasing Psalms is one example. We also meditate on Scripture and absorb its meaning into our hearts.

Journaling

We let our pen be our instrument of rage, of grief, of confusion and sort out our thoughts and feelings this way rather than ventilating on the people around us.

Telephone Calls

We break the isolation by calling another support group member and saying, "I'm feeling confused by what just happened. Do you have a minute to help me work through it?" As receivers of these calls, we try to make time for each other, and when we do, we usually benefit more than the caller.

Confession and Accountability

We believe the popular recovery saying "We are as sick as our secrets." As we reveal our secret behaviors and feelings, we receive God's forgiveness and the acceptance of other group members. Our secrets lose their powerfulness against us when they're shared.

Support Group Meetings

We watch the Holy Spirit become unleashed in our loose band of followers who commit themselves to sharing themselves and accepting what others share no matter what they say. The fact that we're here is a powerful statement that we've broken out of denial and we want to get better. Let's congratulate ourselves for coming!

Sponsoring

We work as a team with other recovering compulsive overeaters who are willing to share their experience, strength, and hope.

Abstinence

We abstain from compulsive overeating by choosing the eating plan that is best for us. We surrender this plan to God daily and ask him to give us the love and care we need for that day.

Service

We abandon our self-obsessed ways and try to practice service that is selfless and that offers us no rewards.

WHAT MAKES A SUPPORT GROUP WORK?

Participation

Support groups help people grow as they share their stories, listen to others, and reflect on what they've said and heard. Everyone should get a chance to contribute, and if you have a lot of people, you may have to ensure that by using the referee's time-out signal when people share over five minutes. If the group finishes early, you can always invite members to share again. Any abstaining compulsive eater may facilitate the group. Encourage others to participate by preparing a group telephone list or setting up chairs.

The sharing goes on and even deepens after and between meetings. A telephone list promotes this "after-hours" activity. Support group members grow from visiting groups like theirs at other churches and from attending workshops and conferences.

As in OA, you may wish to study one Step a month, reading from a book such as *The Twelve Steps of Overeaters Anonymous* or *A Hunger for Healing,* each of which contains a full chapter on each Step. After members take turns reading a page of the chapter, others are invited to comment on the text.

Some groups start out with a planned topic such as honesty or loneliness, which provides a loose structure. If a member has an issue they're struggling with, such as anger or fear, they may share on that topic. It may even get the ball rolling in a direction that meets members' needs better than the planned one.

Organization

Have an announcement printed in the church bulletin inviting potential support group members and their relatives and friends. Make sure that first meeting goes well. Start and finish on time. Make people feel welcome. Choose a room that feels inviting and have printed materials available. Try to have child care available—one of the best things a church can do for its kids is help the kids' parents get into recovery.

Focus

A support group is not a class, although information may be shared. It is not a Bible study, although the Bible is the authority on truth for Christians present. It is not a gripe session, although members may "air dirty laundry." It is not a therapy group, although we do work through experiences. (You may wish to keep a resource list of therapists for those who would like professional help.) It is not a healing session, although we do ask God to give us the hope we need so badly. It is a safe place to share our unhealthy behaviors and what we think is at the root of them and to make ourselves accountable to refocus our negative behaviors by surrendering them to God.

APPENDIX 3

Support Group Resources

I'm thankful that so many resources now exist. Some churches offer their own support groups, but most do not. You may want to consult some of these organizations, although I don't necessarily endorse them.

RESOURCE ORGANIZATIONS

Groups for Compulsive Overeaters

Overeaters Anonymous
World Service Office
P.O. Box 92870
Los Angeles, CA 90009

Groups for Compulsives

Inner Development
P.O. Box 2351
Irwindale, CA 91706

National Association for Christian Recovery
P.O. Box 11095
Whittier, CA 90603

National Association of Anorexia Nervosa and Associated Disorders
P.O. Box 7
Highland Park, IL 60035

Overcomers Outreach, Inc.
2290 West Whittier Blvd.
La Habra, CA 90631

Parents in Recovery
673 Washington Road
Pittsburgh, PA 15228

Secular Organizations for Sobriety (SOS)
P.O. Box 15781
No. Hollywood, CA 91615

Serenity Retreat League
Father Frederick G. Lawrence, S.T.
P.O. Box 10
Stirling, NJ 07980

Sinners Anonymous Service Center
P.O. Box 26001
Austin, TX 78755-0001

Groups for Dysfunctional Family Recovery

Adult Children of Alcoholics
Central Service Board
P.O. Box 3216
Torrance, California 90505

Children of Alcoholics Foundation
200 Park Ave.
New York, NY 10166

National Association for Children of Alcoholics
31706 Coast Highway, Suite 201
South Laguna, CA 92677

PRINT RESOURCES

There are many more books than these, but here are some to whet your appetite. Some are geared specifically to Christians; others are not. If you don't see what you need, check your local bookstore.

Compulsive Eating

B., Bill. *The Compulsive Overeater.* Minneapolis, MN: CompCare Publications, 1981.

L., Elisabeth. *Keep Coming Back.* San Francisco, CA: Harper/Hazelden, 1989.

The Twelve Steps of Overeaters Anonymous. Torrance, CA: Overeaters Anonymous, 1990.

Daily Meditation Books

Johnson, Jan. *Surrendering Hunger: 365 Devotions for Christians Recovering from Eating Disorders.* San Francisco, CA: HarperSanFrancisco, 1993.

Keller, Paul. *God Grant: 365 Christ Centered Daily Meditations for Recovery.* San Francisco, CA: Harper & Row, 1989.

Overeaters Anonymous, Inc. for Today. Torrance, CA: Overeaters Anonymous, 1982.

Stephens, Barbara. *Psalms for Recovery.* San Francisco, CA: HarperSanFrancisco, 1991.

W., Nancy. *On the Path: Affirmations for Adults Recovering from Childhood Sexual Abuse.* San Francisco, CA: HarperSanFrancisco, 1991.

Compulsive Eating and Related Issues

McFarland, Barbara, and Tyeis Baker-Baumann. *Sexuality and Compulsive Eating.* Center City, MN: Hazelden Educational Materials, 1987.

———. *Feeding the Empty Heart: Adult Children and Compulsive Eating.* Center City, MN: Hazelden Educational Materials, 1988.

Compulsive Behavior

Alcoholics Anonymous. *The Twelve Steps and Twelve Traditions.* New York: Alcoholics Anonymous World Services, Inc., 1952.

———. Alcoholics Anonymous [The Big Book]. New York: Alcoholics Anonymous World Services, Inc., 1976.

Carnes, Patrick, Ph.D. *Out of the Shadows: Understanding Sexual Addiction.* Minneapolis, MN: CompCare Publications, 1985.

Friends in Recovery. *The Twelve Steps for Christians.* San Diego, CA: Recovery Publications, 1988.

LeSourd, Sandra Simpson. *The Compulsive Woman.* Old Tappan, NJ: Fleming Revell, 1987.

May, Gerald. *Addiction and Grace.* San Francisco, CA: Harper & Row, 1988.

Miller, Keith. *Hope in the Fast Lane.* San Francisco, CA: Harper & Row, 1987.

———. *A Hunger for Healing.* San Francisco, CA: HarperSanFrancisco, 1991.

Small Group Study Books for Compulsive Eaters

Johnson, Jan. *Eating Disorders: Satisfying the Heart's Hunger.* Littleton, CO: Serendipity House, 1993.

Small Group Study Books for General Compulsive Behavior

Christians in Recovery. *The Twelve Steps—A Spiritual Journey.* San Diego, CA: Recovery Publications, 1988.

W., Claire. *God, Help Me Stop! A Twelve Step Bible Workbook for Recovery from Compulsive Behavior.* San Diego, CA: Books West, 1982, P.O. Box 27364, San Diego, CA 92198.

Dysfunctional Family Recovery

Black, Claudia. *It Will Never Happen to Me: Children of Alcoholics as Youngsters.* Denver, CO: M.A.C. Printing and Publications Division, 1982.

Bradshaw, John. *Homecoming: Reclaiming and Championing Your Inner Child.* New York: Bantam Books, 1990.

Grayson, Curt, and Jan Johnson. *Creating a Safe Place: Christians Healing from the Hurt of Dysfunctional Families.* San Francisco, CA: HarperSanFrancisco, 1991.

Woititz, Janet. *Adult Children of Alcoholics.* Deerfield Beach, FL: Health Communications, 1983.

———. *The Struggle for Intimacy.* Deerfield Beach, FL: Health Communications, 1985.

Wright, Norman J. *Always Daddy's Girl.* Ventura, CA: Regal Books, 1989.

Sexual Abuse

Bass, Ellen, and Laura Davis. *The Courage to Heal: A Guide for Women Survivors of Child Sexual Abuse.* San Francisco, CA: Harper & Row, 1988.

Frank, Jan. *A Door of Hope.* San Bernardino, CA: Here's Life Publishers, 1987.

Spiritual Growth in Dysfunctionality

Johnson, Jan. *When It Hurts to Grow.* Wheaton, IL: Victor Books, 1991.

Seamands, David A. *Healing Memories.* Wheaton, IL: Victor Books, 1985.

———. *Healing for Damaged Emotions.* Wheaton, IL: Victor Books, 1989.

Recovering Parents

O'Gorman, Patricia, and Philip Oliver-Diaz. *Breaking the Cycle of Addiction.* Deerfield Beach, FL: Health Communications, 1987.

Rolfe, Randy Colton. *Adult Children Raising Children.* Deerfield Beach, FL: Health Communications, 1990.

Walker, Ellen. *Growing Up with My Children: Reflections of a Less-Than-Perfect Parent.* Center City, MN: Hazelden Foundation, 1988.

Recovery Magazines

Changes magazine
Health Communications, Inc.
3201 S.W. 15th Street
Deerfield Beach, FL 33442-8124

Lifeline (an international monthly journal of Overeaters Anonymous)
Overeaters Anonymous
P.O. Box 6190
Torrance, CA 90504

STEPS
P.O. Box 11095
Whittier, CA 90603

Notes

INTRODUCTION

1. Douglas Steere, ed., *Thomas Kelly, A Testament of Devotion,* Living Selections from the Great Devotional Classics (Nashville, TN: The Upper Room, 1955), 11.

CHAPTER 1: HUNGRY FOR SOMETHING MORE

1. All names in this book have been changed to protect the anonymity of fellow strugglers.

CHAPTER 2: WHEN EATING TAKES OVER

1. Gerald May, *Addiction and Grace* (San Francisco, CA: Harper & Row, 1988), 18.
2. May, 26ff.
3. Patrick Carnes, *Out of the Shadows* (Minneapolis, MN: CompCare Publications, 1983), 15.
4. Carnes, 120. Dr. Carnes words the fourth belief for the sex addict: "Sex is my most important need." For the compulsive eater, eating is the most important need.
5. Overeaters Anonymous, "In Answer to Your Inquiry," an OA brochure (Torrance, CA: Overeaters Anonymous, 1982), middle inside page.

CHAPTER 3: WHAT ABOUT MY FAITH?

1. Interview with author, licensed family and addiction counselor Father Peter Canavan, S.A.
2. Interview with author, psychologist Dr. Louis Stoetzer.
3. "The Secret of Success: Your Attitude," *Glamour* (June 1989): 240 (compilation—no author given).
4. "Compulsive Overeating and the OA Recovery Program" (Torrance, CA: Overeaters Anonymous, 1981), 10. Used with permission from Overeaters Anonymous, Los Angeles, CA.
5. Interview with author, psychologist Dr. Patrick Carnes.
6. Charles Clayton Morrison, "Adult Teacher" (Sept.–Nov. 1982): 57 (Wheaton, IL: Scripture Press, 1982).

CHAPTER 4: WHAT IT TAKES TO CHANGE

1. May, 28.
2. Madeleine L'Engle, *Walking on Water: Reflections on Faith and Art* (Wheaton, IL: Harold Shaw Publishers, 1980), 161.
3. May, 17.

CHAPTER 5: ABSTINENCE: A TOOL, NOT A GOAL

1. May, 4.

CHAPTER 6: ABSTINENT? WHO, ME?

1. Barbara McFarland and Tyeis Baker-Baumann, *Feeding the Empty Heart: Adult Children and Compulsive Eating* (Center City, MN: Hazelden Educational Materials, 1988), 79.
2. William Cannon, ed., *Selections from Augustine,* Selections from the Great Devotional Classics (Nashville, TN: The Upper Room, 1950), 17.

CHAPTER 9: MAKING FRIENDS WITH FEELINGS

1. Interview with psychiatrist Dr. Edward Khantzian.
2. May, 2.

3. Interview with psychiatrist Dr. Edward Khantzian.
4. Interview with psychiatrist Dr. Edward Khantzian.
5. Interview with psychologist Dr. Peter Robbins.
6. Interview with psychologist Dr. Louis Stoetzer.
7. Interview with psychologist Dr. Patricia O'Gorman.

CHAPTER 10: TELLING MYSELF THE TRUTH

1. Douglas Steere, "Intercession: Caring for Souls," *Weavings* (Mar./Apr. 1989): 16.
2. Benedicta Ward, S.L.G., ed., *The Sayings of the Desert Fathers* (Kalamazoo, MI: Cistercian Publications, 1975), Poemen 183, 162, as cited in Roberta C. Bondi, "Becoming Bearers of Reconciliation," *Weavings* (Jan./Feb. 1990): 14.

CHAPTER 11: WHAT'S BEHIND THE MYTHS?

1. McFarland and Baker-Baumann, 3.
2. Back cover of John Bradshaw, *Bradshaw on: The Family* (Deerfield Beach, FL: Health Communications, 1988), says that 96 percent of families in America are dysfunctional.
3. Curt Grayson and Jan Johnson, *Creating a Safe Place: Christians Healing from the Hurt of Dysfunctional Families* (San Francisco, CA: HarperSan-Francisco, 1991), 23.
4. McFarland and Baker-Baumann, 3.
5. Interview with psychologist Dr. Louis Stoetzer.
6. I did not experience sexual abuse, but it is so common among compulsive eaters of both genders and so rooted in the compulsive eater's neediness that it seemed dishonest to omit sexual abuse from a discussion of the compulsive eaters' childhood issues.
7. Interview with therapist Jan Frank.
8. Interview with therapist Charlene Underhill.
9. Interview with psychiatrist Dr. Edward Khantzian.
10. Interview with therapist Jan Frank.
11. Interview with psychologist Dr. Barbara McFarland.
12. Interview with therapist Jan Frank.
13. Interview with psychologist Dr. Patrick Carnes.

CHAPTER 12: "SOLO" TOOLS OF RECOVERY

1. L'Engle, 162.
2. Douglas Steere, ed., *Selections from the Writings of Bernard of Clairvaux*, Great Devotional Classics (Nashville, TN: The Upper Room, 1975), 26.
3. Thomas a Kempis, *Imitation of Christ Selections* (Wheaton, IL: Tyndale House, 1968), 41.

CHAPTER 13: PARTNERED TOOLS OF RECOVERY

1. Richard Foster, *Celebration of Discipline* (San Francisco, CA: Harper & Row, 1988), 128–129.
2. *Catch the Vision!* by Bill Stearns, IFMA Frontier Peoples Committee, 1990, inside page.

CHAPTER 14: WHEN I'M AT RISK

1. Interview with therapist Charlene Underhill.
2. Interview with psychiatrist Dr. Edward Khantzian.

CHAPTER 15: COMPULSION HOPPING

1. Rolf E. Muuss, "Adolescent Eating Disorder: Bulimia," *Adolescence* 21, no. 82 (Summer 1986): 262.
2. "Medical Report," *Glamour* (Oct. 1988): 284.
3. Interview with psychologist Dr. Patrick Carnes.

CHAPTER 16: DO MY KIDS HAVE TO BE COMPULSIVE EATERS, TOO?

1. Interview with therapist Randy Rolfe.
2. Interview with psychologist Dr. Barbara McFarland.
3. John Bradshaw, as featured in "Homecoming: Reclaiming and Championing Your Inner Child," a video series shown on public broadcasting station KCET, Los Angeles, June 8–9, 1991.
4. Interview with psychologist Dr. Barbara McFarland.
5. Interview with psychologist Dr. Barbara McFarland.
6. Interview with therapist Randy Rolfe.

7. John Bradshaw, KCET.
8. Adapted from Patricia O'Gorman and Philip Oliver-Diaz, *Breaking the Cycle of Addiction* (Deerfield Beach, FL: Health Communications, 1987), 151–152.
9. Interview with therapist Randy Rolfe.
10. Interview with therapist Charlene Underhill.

CHAPTER 17: CHALLENGES OF A GROWING RECOVERY

1. Judith Willis, "The Gender Gap at the Dinner Table," HHS Publication no. 84-2197 (Rockville, MD: Department of Health and Human Services, 1984), 2.
2. Ann Goodman, "A Weighty Issue," *Harper's Bazaar* (Apr. 1988): 207.
3. Brett Silverstein, Lauren Perdue, Barbara Peterson, and Eileen Kelly, "The Role of the Mass Media in Promoting a Thin Standard of Bodily Attractiveness for Women," *Sex Roles* 14, nos. 9/10 (1986): 522–531.
4. Interview with nutritionist Dr. Judith Stern.
5. Janis Jibrin, "Born to Be Fat?" *Family Circle* (July 23, 1991): 44.
6. Jibrin, 44.
7. Interview with nutritionist Dr. Judith Stern.
8. Dr. Judith Stern as quoted in Paul Monarez, "Yo-Yo Cycle Is Tough to Break," *Daily News,* L.A. Life, Monday, Oct. 8, 1990, p. 5.
9. Interview with nutritionist Dr. Judith Stern.
10. Jibrin, 46.
11. Interview with psychologist Dr. Barbara McFarland.
12. McFarland and Baker-Baumann, 43.
13. May, 90.
14. May, 90.
15. Interview with therapist Charlene Underhill.

CHAPTER 18: NEW FREEDOMS IN RECOVERY

1. Interview with psychologist Dr. Barbara McFarland.
2. Interview with psychotherapist Fran Hill.
3. Marshall Cook, *Freeing Your Creativity: A Writer's Guide* (Cincinnati, OH: Writer's Digest Books, 1992), 35.

APPENDIX 1: THE TWELVE STEPS AND TWELVE TRADITIONS OF OVEREATERS ANONYMOUS

1. Permission to use the Twelve Steps of Alcoholics Anonymous for adaptation granted to Overeaters Anonymous by AA World Services, Inc.

   The Twelve Steps of Overeaters Anonymous, as adapted, are reprinted here with the permission of Overeaters Anonymous, Inc. Permission to reprint OA's Twelve Steps does not mean that OA has reviewed or approved the content of this publication or that OA agrees with the views expressed herein.
2. For more information on how Wilson was influenced by the Oxford Group, see Tim Stafford's article, "The Hidden Gospel of the Twelve Steps," *Christianity Today* (July 22, 1991): 14–19.
3. Permission to use the Twelve Traditions of Alcoholics Anonymous for adaptation granted to Overeaters Anonymous by AA World Services, Inc.

   The Twelve Traditions of Overeaters Anonymous, as adapted, are reprinted here with the permission of Overeaters Anonymous, Inc. Permission to reprint OA's Twelve Steps does not mean that OA has reviewed or approved the content of this publication or that OA agrees with the views expressed herein.
4. Condensed from "Overeaters Anonymous: How It Began," by Rozanne S., printed in the OA brochure "To the Newcomer," 11–12.

Subject Index

Biblical Index